T5-BPY-707

RESEARCH ON INSTRUCTION

DESIGN AND EFFECTS

Edited by

**Sanne Dijkstra,
Bernadette H.A.M. van Hout Wolters,
Pieter C. van der Sijde, Editors**

University of Twente, The Netherlands

EDUCATIONAL TECHNOLOGY PUBLICATIONS
ENGLEWOOD CLIFFS, NEW JERSEY

039609

Library of Congress Cataloging-in-Publication Data

Research on instruction : design and effects / edited by Sanne
   Dijkstra, Bernadette H.A.M. van Hout Wolters, Pieter C. van der
   Sijde.
      p. cm.
   Includes bibliographical references.
   ISBN 0-87778-221-0
   1. Instructional systems—Design. 2. Educational technology.
I. Dijkstra, S. II. Hout Wolters, Bernadette H.A.M. van.
III. Sijde, Peter van der.
LB1028.35.R47   1989   89-25682
371.3'078--dc20   CIP

Copyright © 1990 Educational Technology Publications, Inc., Englewood Cliffs, New Jersey 07632.

All rights reserved. No part of this book may be re-
produced or transmitted, in any form or by any
means, electronic or mechanical, including photo-
copying, recording, or by any information storage
and retrieval system, without permission in writing
from the Publisher.

Printed in the United States of America.

Library of Congress Catalog Card Number:
89-25682.

International Standard Book Number:
0-87778-221-0.

First Printing: January 1990.

RESEARCH ON INSTRUCTION

DESIGN AND EFFECTS

ABOUT THE BOOK

This book provides an impression of the progress and advances in the development of instructional design rules and the assessment of their usefulness. All of the authors interpret the effectiveness of instructional variables in the context of a cognitive psychological theory of knowledge acquisition and skill training. The first chapter presents an overview of the key issues.

In the context of the theoretical framework various instructional design rules are described and tested for class and relational concepts, for principles and for problem solving procedures. The subject matter used to study the effects of instruction on knowledge acquisition is borrowed from empirical sciences such as biology and medicine, while the subject matter used to study the effects of instruction on learning to construct problem solving procedures is adopted from computer science.

The chapters pay attention to several instructional variables, including attribute and paragraph isolation with color; nature and number of examples for teaching concepts; strategies in example presentation for programming instruction; time spent on the components of a teaching script and decision models for determining the successive instructive message. Attention also is given to the role of the computer for the improvement of learning. A whole chapter is devoted to the development of an instructional design expert system.

The final chapter presents a global overview of the description of knowledge and skills for purpose of instruction.

PREFACE

The label "Instructional Technology" was introduced in the period between 1960 and 1970 to give a description of methods (or procedures) of instruction to promote the acquisition of knowledge and cognitive skills. In the United States of America these methods were strongly influenced by the ideas of behaviorism. In the same period, instructional technology attracted attention in the Soviet Union, where Landa developed his method of algorithmization of instruction. Because of several shortcomings of the technology which showed up when the latter was used, it soon became clear that further development of both the theory and technology of instruction was necessary. This need was underlined by the early examples of the application of the computer in education.

A decade later, Gagné and Briggs introduced the label "Instructional Design". Their "Principles of Instructional Design" showed the influence of the emerging field of cognitive psychology on the description of the varieties of learning and the analysis of the learning task. This trend resulted in more contributions addressing the problems of instruction. In 1978 Glaser edited the first volume of "Advances in Instructional Psychology". In this volume the authors make clear that the study of the acquisition of complex human behavior in instructional settings will contribute both to the theory of knowledge acquisition within a science of cognition and to the technology of instruction.

Meanwhile, instructional design principles were being further developed. In 1983 Reigeluth edited the first collection of contributions completely dedicated to instructional design theories and models. In 1986 he followed this with "Instructional Theories in Action", in which the theories and models were now applied to the design of lessons. Another volume on instructional design, edited by Jonassen, appeared in 1988. This book focussed on instructional design principles for microcomputer use.

The use of the computer as a means to present instructions fostered both the development of instructional design theories and the experimental and empirical validation of design principles. Intelligent tutoring systems are typical of this development, in which systems instructions and feedback are generated on the basis of a computational model. The model is based on "knowledge" of the subject matter and of the students' learning process and "expertise" in instructional methods. Various intelligent systems have been developed (see Wenger, 1987, for a detailed overview).

The contributions in this book not only present their (interpretation of an) instructional design theory, but they also apply it in experiments in order to evaluate the practical implications. In other words, the usefulness of the instructional design principles is tested experimentally. For a quick overview of the contributions we refer to Table 1 in Chapter 1 (p. 10).

Most of the contributions in this volume have been written by members of the faculty of the University of Twente, the Netherlands. Between 1970 and 1980 the University, aware of the importance of educational technology, laid the foundations for a School of Education emphasizing technological responses to educational problems. A division of Instructional Technology was incorporated in this and became operational in 1982. Profs. Warries and Dijkstra were appointed to develop a research programme in cooperation with other staff members of the division. The content of this volume is part of the results of this endeavor. Two visiting scholars from the United States of America, Profs. Merrill and Tennyson, also contributed.

Without the assistance of several specialists the editors would have been unable to finish all the work necessary in the publication of this volume. They thus wish to thank Glen Leblanc and Anne-Moon van Hest for linguistic editing. Their thanks also go to Marion Davina and Thyra Kuijpers, both of the division of Instructional Technology of the University of Twente, for typing and editorial assistance and to Maria Driessen for preparing the diagrams.

University of Twente, The Netherlands

Sanne Dijkstra
Bernadette H.A.M. van Hout Wolters
Pieter C. van der Sijde

CONTENTS

Preface

0396096

1

THEORY AND THE SYSTEMATIC DESIGN OF INSTRUCTION

Egbert Warries
University of Twente

ABSTRACT

To introduce the following chapters, an overview of the projects is given in terms of methods, intended outcomes, and conditions of instruction. Meta-theoretical reflections are presented about the meaning of theory for the systematic design of instruction. It is argued that there is a need for an independent theory of instruction, which can advance the work and identity of the academic community of instructional designers. Five criteria are defined which a theory of instruction has to meet.

THE OBJECT OF STUDY FOR SCIENTISTS, AN EXAMPLE

Instructional theory suffers from the fact that its object of study is a man-made system which differs with the intentions and expertise of the maker. Instructional scientists envy researchers from other disciplines, who have no doubts whatsoever about the identity of their object of study. Scientists such as biologists or astronomers when observing what is happening in nature and in the universe seem to have certainties that are beyond reach for instructional researchers.

Some years ago a Dutch television network, KRO, (1983) broadcast a film about a group of biologists who for a long period of time had observed a colony of starlings living in their natural habitat near the sea on the Isle of Schiermonnikoog, one of the lovely Frisian islands north of the mainland. The biologists were interested in the feeding habits of the birds. They suspected that the better food for the young was to be found in fields further away from the nests, and they were anxious to know what the birds would do to solve the problem posed by food quality and flight distance. They guessed that, as the parent birds have a very tight daily schedule, they had to make a choice between enough food of lesser quality and lesser food of excellent quality. From their hiding places and with the use of automatic cameras the biologists carefully recorded under which conditions the observed animals got their food, how many and what type of bugs and grubs the industrious parent birds collected for their offspring, the distance between the searching area and the nests, the feeding pattern, and the physical condition of the young.

For an instructional designer interested in theory development and sometimes asking himself and others what his own object of study must be, the aforementioned project presented a fine example of the first stages in theorizing, after the object of study has been defined. Early in the scientific process, the researcher observes the phenomena, and tries to test hypotheses or to discover new principles. In this case the object of study was limited to one group of starlings, conceived of as an interdependent, separate and representative unit. In the film the project was presented as an exploratory study. The researchers were, in an open-minded way, looking for factors influencing the meals and well-being of the young birds, of which they even analyzed the excrements. They knew and further explored the relevant variables like vegetation, distances to different feeding places, and quantity of food transported by the parents. What they didn't know with enough certainty was the direction and strength of the relationships between the different variables. They were surprised, in the end, to find that the birds appeared to practice a clever compromise between too heavy a work load for themselves and too many seemingly laxative bugs for their young. The object of study was well-defined by the biologists. They knew what they were studying.

The same goes for astronomers, as we may notice when we read about their work. Astronomers know what they are studying. Their scientific community also knew how to change the object of study at the moment when more knowledge about the main variables and phenomena was collected and when better instruments for observation became available. The astronomers of former centuries studied the celestial bodies as seen with the naked eye or through primitive instruments. They looked at the sky and tried to figure out shapes, colors, movements. They guessed or crudely measured distances between the earth and the stars and between different stars. But in our days astronomers know more and have better equipment. They observe the stars and also explore the geological composition and chemical characteristics of celestial bodies. No longer all of the astronomers are working on distances and movements. We might say that it is no longer the stars they are studying but the composition of the stars. It appears, then, that the object of study can change.

What can the instructional theorist or designer learn from biology, astronomy, and other sciences that could be useful for the theory of instruction? Although these sciences differ from instructional science because they are not dealing with man-made objects but with nature, they still teach us that it pays to have an observable and well-defined object of study, even when it is necessary to exchange the old object of study for a new one. These sciences can further tell us that we must not only envy them but we must also adopt their approach and try to define our own object of study and translate results from other sciences into instructional terminology.

THEORY AND DESIGN THEORY

In this chapter we are supposed to present an introduction to the book. We will do so, but we will extend our task a bit. We also offer the reader some meta-theoretical considerations that we judge appropriate for an introduction to the work presented in the following chapters. In particular, we wish to draw attention to the distinction between the general concept "instructional theory" and the more specific concept "instructional design theory". We will stress the distinction between the two because instructional science has a capacity which biology and astronomy do not possess, namely the capacity to manipulate or engineer its object. It is true that biology is gradually getting this capacity as well, but still there is one great difference, besides the difference in scale: for instructional theory the manipulation of the system can be considered the ultimate goal. Our definition of instruction itself is: "Bringing about by means of a well-defined method, that, under given conditions, a learner within a system, will reach a predefined goal". In our paper we will concentrate on the general concept of instructional theory, which is more related to *understanding* than to *improving*. We will treat instructional theory as a general theory dealing with all instructional procedures on a microlevel. This theory consists of propositions about the instructional system (the place where instruction takes place) in general. The general theory that we have in mind does not contain rules for the design of instructional systems nor does it prescribe the behavior of teachers in schools. We could call such a theory a *descriptive* theory, although all theories by nature are descriptive.

Instructional design theories, on the other hand, give rules or principles for the design of instruction. In a few cases they intend also to provide teachers with prescriptions. Over the last ten years design theories or models of instruction have become more and more important for the work of professional, full-time instructional designers. Although design theories frequently refer to descriptive theory or present relevant propositions (often originating from learning theory), their main function is to tell the designer how to design and how to produce courses and lessons.

In this paper we will offer a few comments on the chapters to follow and we try to convince the reader that the development of a general or descriptive theory of instruction is worth striving for. We try to be clear about such a theory by offering five conditions which we think are crucial to the development and growth to maturity of the theory. We prefer to speak of a "true theory of instruction". This is to distinguish it on the one hand from the prescriptive or design theories and on the other hand from the collection of theoretical principles which are applied by instructional designers but originate from disciplines other than instruction. We will now continue our paper with some reflections about the question already touched upon; what the object of study for an instructional theory should be.

Other sciences can be envied by instructional theorists. Empirical sciences, after observing the physical world or the part of it under consideration, order and classify variables and explain and predict phenomena. They apparently know which part of the physical world they are studying: they know what their object of study is. However, as we said, instructional theory suffers from the fact that the object of study is a man-made system. The system is studied in order to improve it. For clarity of thought we had better make a distinction now between the theorists (who study it) and the designers (who improve it). We may notice that designers need knowledge about the system they have to develop or to improve, both in their problem-defining stage and when they are ready to design and produce blueprints for instruction. They do not care where the knowledge, the theory, comes from, as long as it contains variables which can be manipulated. Variables belong to the system in which the instruction takes place: the classroom for children or adults and the interactive situation where learners take individualized lessons. The theorists have to provide the knowledge.

Many theorists and researchers see as the object of study for instructional theory not the instructional system but specific parts of the system. They have chosen the learner, the teacher or the media as their exclusive target. Nowadays probably a majority of the instructional theorists feel themselves part of the growing cognitivist tradition and claim that the object of study is the learning or problem-solving organism, that the relevant variables are to be found in the memory structure and that the cognitive processes form the relevant phenomena. This prevailing cognitivist view seems fine for learning psychologists, but makes things rather difficult for the designers of instruction, because it is the job of the designer to manipulate method variables and mostly he cannot detect method variables in cognitive theory or cannot translate the results from cognitive science into instructional method terminology.

Designers of instruction might feel disappointed and left alone by the theorists. But they must not forget that many efforts have been made to find a theoretical basis for the design of instruction or to promote normative or design theories to the status of real theories.

For a long time now, influential instructional designers have worked from the conviction that a theoretical basis for designing was to be found *outside instruction*. In the writings of Glaser (1966), Merrill (1968), and Snelbecker (1974), it is implicit that the design of instruction is not based on or related to an autonomous body of knowledge about instructional phenomena, but on psychological learning theory. Bruner (1966) and Gagné (1976) hypothesize a very strong bond between theories of learning on the one hand and a normative or prescriptive theory of instruction on the other hand. In their opinion, there are theoretical notions from psychology that have to be directly applied by the teacher when designing and delivering instruction.

It may be true that in the future many practical instruction rules or principles will be derived directly or indirectly from learning theory and can be used by professional designers. But it seems difficult to think of the cognitive explanations of instructional phenomena (like concept learning or Gagné's instructional events in the classroom) as contributions to a true instructional theory in the sense that we have in mind. Research resulting in explanations for phenomena by referring to other theories does not contribute to the theory at hand. It could even lead to an ongoing reduction (in the case of instruction, even going far beyond cognitive science), and lead the instructional theorist far away from his proper object of study.

But there are also some successful *normative* theories. They are brought together in a fine collection by Reigeluth (1983b). In the first chapter of this "green book" he edited (Reigeluth, 1983a), distinguishes between descriptive and prescriptive theory, but he does not seem to distinguish between instructional theory and the design theories. We may conclude that in his view the instructional models that he admitted as chapters in his book, together *are* the theory of instruction. This conclusion is corroborated when we read in the "yellow book" of Reigeluth (1987) that a descriptive theory of instruction "describes the effect of a whole model of instruction", which suggests that the prescription came before the description. Reigeluth (1983a) distinguishes further between instructional design as a professional activity and instructional design as a discipline and then he gives a description of such a discipline. He sees the discipline as "concerned with producing knowledge about optimal "blueprints"-knowledge about diverse methods of instruction, optimal combinations of methods (i.e. whole models), and situations in which each of those models is optimal." This is a typical normative notion of instructional theory, and a way of thinking comparable to what teacher educators state about optimal teacher behavior in the so-called "teachers should" statements. The question however is, if there will ever be developed a prescriptive theory for all types of outcomes, working under all types of conditions for instructional designers.

Contrary to the standpoint of Reigeluth and other writers on design theory, one must conclude that in the end normative theories are not sufficient as tools for instructional designers. Designers need not only access to design rules or complete normative models, but they also need a descriptive instructional theory. We believe that there is a "raison d'être" for what one could call a true or descriptive theory of instruction. Such a theory possesses the same general goals and functions that all other theories or disciplines have. All theories classify, order, explain and predict the phenomena in the physical world or in man-made systems. In the case of instruction it is the instructional system.

IS THERE A THEORY OF INSTRUCTION?

The following question arises: Does such a theory already exist in the professional field of instruction? Before trying to answer this question, we may observe that *if* an instructional theory, or an instructional science, in this sense, does exist, it must be young, even in comparison with rather new disciplines like sociology or psychology. Therefore such a science or theory must be in one of the earliest of those stages that all empirical theories must pass through during their development and growth to maturity. These stages are, in roughly the following sequence:

(1)   Interesting phenomena are noticed and preliminary boundaries are set out, delineating the domain or object or system in which these phenomena must be studied.
(2)   Variables discernible within the phenomena in the domain are given names and classified in taxonomies.
(3)   Phenomena are systematically observed and recorded either in natural settings or in experiments.
(4)   A methodology for analysis and synthesis of the collected data is developed and recognized.
(5)   Data analyses having taken place, principles and laws governing the phenomena are formulated and gradually built into a body of integrated knowledge.
(6)   Hypotheses are derived from what is known and then tested and rejected or accepted and added to the body of knowledge.

The question was whether a descriptive theory of instruction does exist. At first sight one feels inclined to answer this question negatively, because there does not seem to be general recognition of such a descriptive theory. But, on closer investigation, limiting ourselves to the mainstream of instructional design literature, one notices in the well-known design theories (Reigeluth 1983b, 1987) many descriptive components, stated in instructional terminology.

Many models contain descriptive, or in our sense real theoretical, propositions pertaining e.g. to the taxonomy of method- and outcome-variables and the phenomena taking place in instruction. The fact that these models have these descriptive components is to be hailed because in this way a common language becomes available for instructional designers. The language makes it possible to communicate about the instructional system which designers are to improve. These descriptive components of the models also provide the means for a deeper understanding of the rules offered by the model. This understanding is essential for professional designers, in the many cases where no model gives them the precise design rules and where they have to take their own decisions about design problems.

Often the descriptive components are defined in the language of other disciplines, sometimes untranslatable and sometimes apt to be transposed into instructional variables. If we also bear in mind that many earlier authors have written about instructional theory without mentioning it (like Carroll, 1963; Bloom, 1976; Gage, 1978), one could conclude that there is more theory about structure and functioning of the instructional system than many of us recognize. Therefore in the last analysis the answer must be affirmative. There does exist a descriptive instructional theory "avant la lettre", a family of scattered, unintegrated, implicitly mentioned statements, of paradigms and incomplete theories, often stated in terms derived from other disciplines.

Wouldn't it be better then to keep things as they are or seem to grow, and consider instructional theory as a normative theory that both understands (a little) and improves (much)? Would a combination of designing and understanding not be the hallmark of academic designing? Maybe it would, but the risk is very great that the theory will become or remain a cookbook theory with more prescribing than understanding. No, we believe that the professional activity of instructional design can benefit from a sharper distinction between a body of knowledge called "instructional theory" (others would prefer the label "instructional science") and the collection of models or design theories of a more normative character.

UNDERSTANDING SYSTEMS: THREE MAIN VARIABLES

The goal of all scientific enterprise is understanding. When we understand a man-made system or a part of the physical world, we are able to explain phenomena and to predict new phenomena. This also holds for research on instruction. The goal of instructional theory is understanding the instructional system. For a theory of man-made systems, the rationale, the necessity and even the survival of the theory all lie in the circumstance that understanding the system is prerequisite for improving the system. It is no coincidence that the two concepts are often mentioned together. In his definition of instructional design theory, Reigeluth (1983a) uses the expression "a discipline that is concerned with understanding and improving the process of instruction". This definition may be appropriate when applied to models containing both theoretical (descriptive) elements and normative (prescriptive) elements, but the definition does not fit with the common descriptive conception of scientific theory. Does that matter for the designer? We believe it does.

We believe that it can be wholesome for instructional design as a professional activity, if theorists strive for understanding and if they write in accordance with it. Although the ultimate function of a theory might be improvement, understanding is the immediate goal which the theorist must constantly have in mind during theory development.

Conceiving of theories as distinct from design theories seems highly defensible if we think in system terms and consider all instruction taking place in man-made systems. Existing systems can be improved and new ones designed, only if the phenomena that take place in the system are well understood. That is the case when we are able to explain the phenomena and to predict them in terms referring to the system. In other words, only if we are able to relate changes in one component or variable of the system to changes in another component or variable of the same system, do we understand the system or a part of it. In the systematic approach, or in instructional system development, understanding the system has to be considered basic to improving the system. And understanding a system means having defined the variables and knowing about the direction and strength of the relations between the variables of the system.

But what are the right terms and main variables in an instructional system? Reigeluth (1983a, 1986) distinguishes three types of main variables: methods, outcomes, and conditions. In experimental psychology we are familiar with the distinction and the relationship between independent and dependent variables. Bloom (1981) uses the term "alterable variables" in his plea to concentrate research efforts in education on variables which can be controlled and manipulated. In his view, the research on such variables enables researchers and educators "to move from emphasis on prediction and the classification of students to a concern for causality and the relations between means and ends in teaching and learning". In research on instruction, it is customary to call the variables that are the "independent" ones the method variables. Thus we have two important components in the instructional system, the *method variables* and the effect variables or *outcomes*. In addition, in man-made systems there is a third group of highly relevant main variables or parameters: the *conditions* or constraints of the system. In research on instruction the importance of the conditions can hardly be overestimated. Conditions have an impact on the direction and strength of the method/outcomes relation. Instructional systems can be very productive under given conditions, and become unproductive or counter-productive when conditions change or become less favorable.

The relationship between these three components in instructional systems reveals itself in a statement of the following general form: Under conditions X, method Y is related to outcome Z. A scientist stating propositions of this type demonstrates understanding of the system or part of it. Again Reigeluth (1983a) points out the specific role of the designer. When a designer tries to improve an existing system or tries to set up a new system or, more generally, tries to solve an instructional problem, he will in certain stages of the design process use the available knowledge about this system type, and try to vary the method variables in such a way and toward such values that he gets the desired outcomes. We leave undecided the question if these system outcomes must always be learning outcomes. And we leave untreated the question what else the designer must do during his work as a designer, next to manipulating the method-variables.

THE CHAPTERS OF THIS BOOK AND THE MAIN VARIABLES

In Table 1 the contents of the separate chapters are classified under the three main variables of instructional theory. In the last column of the table an indication is given of the function of each chapter and its implications for the instructional theory or the instructional design theory. In this section we will first discuss the methods, outcomes and conditions of the chapters in a general sense. Then we will comment on each of the chapters separately.

Our first general comment concerns the methods used. From the table it becomes clear that a heterogeneous collection of method-variables is reported on in these twelve chapters. The method-variables pertain to characteristics of group instruction, prototype theory as a method, advance organizer, color in media, form, number and range of examples, teacher training and a new method to teach computer programming. The many-sided collection represents instruction in daily life as it were, where also many different methods are used. In a single case the instructional method is made mathematically explicit, in order to manipulate the method-variable in decision-theoretical terms. Partly the research is testing hypotheses in the classical sense, using control groups, partly the research is testing the method: does the method work? Is the hypothesized relationship between method-variable and outcome variable present? Three chapters are of a more theoretical nature: Merrill, Tennyson, and Dijkstra.

What kind of outcomes are measured in research on instruction? In instruction it is always tempting to regard achievement test scores as the sole form of outcomes. Indeed, from the list in this table it can be seen that cognitive outcomes form the majority. But fortunately there are also outcomes in the list, which can be categorized as process variables, and there are affective outcomes. In several chapters the knowledge and use of concepts form the outcome variables. In several chapters the mastery of concepts is measured by reproduction and classification tasks.

What type of constraints or conditions for instruction do we find in the following chapters? Several authors committed themselves to real-life concepts for their design on concept instruction. These concepts, as is known, have the drawback of familiarity and preconceptions for the students participating in the experiments. The authors managed to overcome that difficulty. Here again we have a real life-situation. Many different conditions are given in the various chapters. One of them is the population the researcher is dealing with; for some of the chapters students in higher professional education, for others adults in their working environment. Sometimes it is the equipment in use, sometimes the condition is the available time for instruction. As in professional designing practice, the conditions often seem

Table 1
The Main Instructional Variables and the Contribution of Each Chapter

CHAPTER AUTHORS	METHODS	OUTCOMES	CONDITIONS	CONTRIBUTION
Merrill & Li	-strategies -transactions -content structure -course organization	-concept classifications -procedures for device operation	-goals of instruction -situation -audience -(content structure) -(course organization)	-theory of instruction -tool for design
Van Merriënboer & Krammer	-completion-strategy	-student achievement: declarative, procedural	-program COMAL -high school students	-design rules
Van der Sijde	-script training	-cognitive skill -classroom processes -student achievement: declarative	-short training -high school teachers	-scientific basis for the art of the design of teaching
Van Hout Wolters et al	-colouring instructional texts	-student achievement: declarative -student appreciation	-instruction by text -students in nursing school	-design rules for instructional texts
Rakers et al	-advance organizer	-student achievement: declarative, procedural	-image workpiece -operating program -student lathe operators -professional skill	-design tactics
Tennyson	-delivery -instructional variables -instructional strategies	-storage of knowledge: declarative, procedural, contextual -retrieval	-computers, (MAIS) -training objectives -knowledge base	-theory role of media
Gulmans	-filmed proto-types	-diagnostic skill, concept classification	-students in nursing school -professional skill	-confirmation of Tennyson's theory -design rules for instruction of diagnostic skill
Leemkuil	-number and heterogeneity of examples	-student achievement: declarative, procedural	-ecological validity -school subject matter -natural concepts -sixth grade students	-design rules biology
Ranzijn	-form of example presentation	-student achievement: declarative, procedural	-video (real life) -natural concepts -high school students	-design rules for instruction by prototypes
Vos	-instance practicing in program controlled CAI	-student achievement -program control	-MAIS program controlled	-design rules for CAI
Dijkstra	-define knowledge and skills -present knowledge -demonstrate skill	-student achievement	-knowledge construction -authentic activity of students	-cognitive theory -instruction design theory

to have been given first and then the methods were chosen to archieve the intended outcomes.

Chapter 2: Merrill & Li describe their plans for an expert system, to be consulted by designers during an early stage in the development process. In most Instructional Development Models there is a phase preceding prototype-construction. This preceding stage, resulting in blueprints for the lessons to be constructed, could be seen as the phase of design-proper. Merrill & Li's expert system prompts the designer to use what they call "seasoned instructional design principles" for this stage: the use of strategies, transactions and typecasting of content structure and course organization, in order to obtain instructional goals like concept classification and the correct performance of operational skills. Rules apply under specified conditions. Like most of the chapters in this book, this one is about individualized instruction. The chapter's contribution lies in the fact that it not only provides a tool for designers but also gives us an excellent description of phenomena taking place in an instructional system.

Chapter 3: Van Merriënboer & Krammer studied the interaction in groups of high school students learning to program in COMAL. They designed an instructional method in the form of a "completion strategy", using a selection of existing instructional tactics. The tactics and strategy were chosen in order to reach outcomes comprising declarative and procedural knowledge. From their experiments the authors draw conclusions about the merits of design rules based upon this completion method, in comparison with the common instructional strategy in which the student must generate a completely new computer program. They studied the influence of the completion strategy on verbal interaction among the students. As a psychological sideline they also explored whether their method gave better results for impulsive students. For the design of programming courses for this important target population their work seems an innovative contribution.

Chapter 4: Van der Sijde designed and evaluated a training course on classroom behavior for high school mathematics teachers. For practical reasons the course had to be very short. The course content consisted of a script of teacher activities during one classroom hour and a set of management prescriptions originating from Kounin, who originally induced these from his observations of teachers. Two experiments were carried out: one to test if the trainees performed according to the taught script and the management rules, and one to test the achievement of the students. The intended outcomes of the instruction encompassed both process and effect variables. This type of research and the resulting prototype training course can both be seen as a contribution to the scientific basis for the art of designing classroom instruction.

Chapter 5: In an experiment with first-year students in a nursing college, Van Hout Wolters et al. investigated whether the use of colour for structuring the chapters in a textbook is positively evaluated by students and whether this colouring enhances retention of information. From the literature it is known that operators in industry prefer coloured screens and that young children more easily learn better to read from coloured books. The authors asked themselves if the same affective and cognitive outcomes will be reached if colour printing is applied in instructional texts for apprentice nurses. They used colour to emphasize important subsections in nursing texts like "diagnosis" and "treatment" of disorders. The use of colour to isolate and indicate such important and recurrent aspects of informative text, comparable to slots in schemata, seemed promising. They also investigated the role of individual differences.

Chapter 6: Rakers et al., after applying an advance organizer in their instructional design, tested the performance of student operators in programming computer numerically controlled (CNC) machines in industry. They compare performance on a conventional programming task with performance in a condition where instruction starts with an organizer. In their discussion they propose some instructional tactics to improve the results of the course they evaluated. They pay attention to the difference between declarative and procedural knowledge in programming skills and the common knowledge base in the student for both the image of the work piece and the program to execute the task. Their work is a contribution of instructional design to the problems faced by trainers in modernizing industry.

Chapter 7: Tennyson describes how, in the delivery phase, computers (in particular the Minnesota Adaptive Instructional System, MAIS) can enhance the quality of instruction. He relates media or media-based instructional variables to learning types and traces them to declarative, procedural and what he calls contextual knowledge. He concentrates on the variables and strategies that he and his associates studied for more than fifteen years. Delivery methods, it is aruged in this chapter, have to meet two criteria: they must exhibit a direct trace to a specific learning process and there must be empirical evidence for their significance. Although the first criterion seems to conflict with what we say in this chapter about the autonomy of a theory of instruction, the second criterion clearly supports our point of view. Several other authors in this volume refer to Tennyson's other writings, on concept learning.

Chapter 8: Gulmans conducted an intriguing experiment on the instruction of concepts. The concept to be mastered was the professional skill of paramedic personnel to diagnose shock. He used well-defined types of shock, to be diagnosed by students in a nursing school. He compared a course that used filmed prototypes to teach different types of shock with a course that presented definitions of the different shock types (and lists of attributes) to the students. The results, favoring the prototype instruction, are explained referring to the better mental image of the shock types and the superior retention of such an image in comparison with propositional knowledge about shock types. His results are a confirmation of Tennyson's theory on concept instruction mentioned in this volume and present a contribution to the design of instruction.

Chapter 9: Leemkuil designed a short CAI-course to teach biology concepts to sixth grade students. He presented videotaped examples of windflowers (of which the pollen does not need to be transported by bees or butterflies) and tested hypotheses about the influence of number and heterogeneity of examples on the development of a cognitive model in the students. His findings regarding the instruction of natural concepts in schools are an interesting contribution to instructional design.

Chapter 10: Ranzijn also used flower types as natural concepts. He studied the learning of concepts in biology classes in high school, as influenced by the way the examples were presented to the students. As an approximation to real-life examples he used video. The other presentation mode was line drawings of the different flower types. For the measurement of outcomes of instruction, declarative knowledge (attributes of the concept) and classification skill were used. The results are to be interpreted as a contribution to the instructional theory about prototype learning.

Chapter 11: Vos, making use of Bayesian decision theory, developed rules for the optimal number of interrogatory examples in the instruction of concepts in Tennyson's Minnesota Adaptive Instructional System. Adapting to students' performance the decision rules proposed by Vos provide for decisions about practicing instances. His rules for program-controlled instruction also take account of the cumulative data from all students taught by the system in the past.

Chapter 12: Dijkstra sketches a general framework for the design of instruction. His paper focuses on the idea, that learning must be an authentic act. Knowledge must not be transferred to the learner but has to be constructed by the learner. After first presenting the taxonomies of instructional content and levels of knowledge, he offers a new subject-matter categorization system. He pays much attention to the difference between knowledge and skill and refers to both Landa and J. Anderson to make clear what his framework is about. The chapter also offers instructional methods, following from knowledge theory. In short, a design should first define knowledge and skills, and then present knowledge and demonstrate skills, before the authentic activity of the student can take place.

THEORIES DON'T PRESCRIBE; THEY DESCRIBE

There is a widespread belief that instructional theory has to be prescriptive. The origin of this belief probably dates back to the beginning of the century, both in Europe and in The United States, and stemmed from the view that the newly gained psychological knowledge could and had to be applied by teachers in elementary schools. Because teachers were not knowledgeable in this field, psychological knowledge had to be translated into prescriptions for the behavior of teachers. Much later Bruner (1966) stated the need for a prescriptive theory, based on learning theory. He called this prescriptive theory an instructional theory and presented the criteria that such a theory had to meet. The prescriptions that Bruner had in mind were meant for teachers. In our view, however, prescriptions in the Brunerian sense are of limited value to designers of instruction.

Prescriptions for teachers have a function different from that of design rules for instruction. Design rules provide options for the designer. Prescriptions must be followed. There is risk involved in prescribing. The prescriptions can be faulty or they can be misunderstood by teachers. However, the risk is not very great. Firstly, teachers, being experienced professionals, are resistant to faulty guidelines given by theorists. Secondly, teachers tend not to interpret and go deeply into the psychological theory behind the prescriptions. Teachers can use prescriptions perfectly well, because the risk of actually following the wrong prescriptions or misinterpretation of the right prescriptions is minimal. But instructional designers do not need prescriptions.

What instructional designers do need (next to design theories) is a sound knowledge of the structure and functioning of the instructional system. Designing is like engineering. Engineering is more than following prescriptions. Engineering is also more than the application of science. It is a method, an attitude, a specialism, and a professional activity which can only be practised on an academic level when the engineer has a thorough knowledge of the system he is developing or improving. It is this knowledge that we draw attention to in this chapter. The instructional designer needs this knowledge to fall back on, in the frequent cases where the design rules, strategies, design theories or his experience do not provide him with the information for taking decisions about steps in the development process. The task of the instructional designer differs widely from the pre-instructional task of the teacher. The designer has to be far more explicit and complete in his developmental work, because the person who will use his product is the learner, and not a specialist who could make up for errors and omissions.

Being explicit and complete presupposes being knowledgeable. The designer must have at his disposal, in his head or easily accessible on the shelf, enough theoretical knowledge about the instructional system to compensate for the errors and omissions in the design theory from which he picks his rules. It is important to note that *making use of knowledge* is quite different from both application of science and following prescriptions. For the designer, it is not the theory which, from the top down, prescribes or is applied, but it is he himself who seeks counsel of or refers to the theory to find a solution for his problem. And, he can only predict effective solutions for his instructional problem if he knows the phenomena in the system. In other words: ... if he has at his disposal a descriptive theory of the instructional system. In the next section we will state three general principles that we judge natural for all theories and also for an instructional theory, and we will give five criteria to measure the healthy development of a theory of instruction. But first we give two reasons why an instructional theory has to be a *descriptive* theory.

Instructional theories are descriptions of reality. They have to be, for two reasons. The first is that instructional theory as a scientific discipline and a means of communication can develop and survive only if instructional theorists conform to the general rules of disciplinary research, which means that they describe what is directly or indirectly observable, and explain and predict phenomena. The other reason is the acceptability for professional designers, of the prescriptions or design rules that accompany, follow from, or refer to the theory. Professional designers need a sound theoretical basis, otherwise they will not (or should not) follow the design rules but behave in accordance with their own intuition or experiential wisdom.

Instructional designers are engineers. They have to plan in advance, foresee what happens during instruction, and produce stand-alone prototypes of instructional programs. They cannot adapt intuitively to the situation at hand as teachers do during their lessons. Therefore designers ask for two types of information: design rules and knowledge about the system. The rules are in some way (not through derivation) linked to and based on propositions in the descriptive theory. Often however, the design rules for instruction are absent or have a strongly heuristic character. Then, in order to take decisions about the method of instruction, designers need a theory which describes the phenomena of the instructional system that they must manipulate. That descriptive theory is the actual theory and we call it *the true theory of instruction* (TTI). We would like to state here that a true theory of instruction must in any case be a descriptive theory which gives the designer an insight in what is known about the phenomena taking place in the instructional system. We have to abandon the idea that an instructional theory should prescribe. Theories don't prescribe, they describe.

A TRUE THEORY OF INSTRUCTION

There are three general principles that we judge natural for all theories and thus also for instructional theory: *Clarity, Autonomy,* and *Economy.*

A theory must be clear about its object of study, the type of phenomena to be studied, the language it will use and the extrinsic goal of the theory. Especially for a theory on man-made systems it is mandatory to describe unambiguously the nature of the system which is to be studied. It must not happen that some researchers believe that the system is the student and others remain convinced that the system is the classroom. In practice a theory must define a fixed object of study and develop and use one language.

Further, a theory must be autonomous in decisions on the identification of its object, its boundaries, the problems to be solved, the training of its theorists, and the research program for the future.

Finally, a theory must economize in its research program. Not everything can be investigated. Some problems are insoluble or finding a solution would cost too much. Some problem types are not situated within the domain (or object) of study. Restrictions have to be made in the choice of the variables to be considered part of the theory.

In the case of instructional theory the principles of clarity, autonomy, and economy for the development of theories lead us to the following five criteria. All efforts to develop a true theory of instruction have to meet these criteria.

(1) All variables in a TTI are instructional variables

Elaboration: A theory of instruction must explain and predict phenomena in instructional systems. These phenomena must be described in terms of relationships between three classes of instructional variables: conditions, methods, outcomes. This is not always easy. Particularly outcomes are often measured in variables from psychology. Researchers have to resist the temptation of explaining phenomena by reference to other fields; all explanatory propositions should be testable through experimentation within the instructional setting using instructional variables. Instructional theorists must study the phenomena in instructional systems, not in the adjacent physiological, psychological or teaching system. They must also make themselves clear to others about their object of study.

(2) The method variables of a TTI are controllable variables

Elaboration: No theory on phenomena in the field of education and training can study everything. A TTI should only study phenomena which can be expressed as relationships between on the one hand, controllable, "alterable" variables and on the other effect-variables or outcomes. This restriction guarantees a lasting bond with existing and future design theories on instruction. It is the designers' job to manipulate the method variables. The propositions designers are interested in are those that state the relationship between method and outcomes, under specified conditions. They cannot do anything with variables which they cannot change, like socio-economical status or innate characteristics of the students. Therefore a TTI occupies itself exclusively with controllable variables in the instructional system.

(3) The method variables of a TTI are paying variables

Elaboration: Here is another restriction on the kind of variables a TTI studies. Only variables which a designer can use are relevant for a theory of instruction. One can think of method variables which are controllable but not cost-effective (paying, remunerative) enough to keep the interest of designers.

Those will disappear. Others, which from a practical standpoint are worth-while, will survive.

(4) A TTI develops a consistent language

Elaboration: A theory is also a means of communication. It is a language and has to be very clear. A theory of instruction must utilize instructional terms, which means that each key concept can be classified into one of the three main categories of variables: conditions, methods, outcomes. In many publications on instruction the terminology is derived from psychology. In some cases it is evident that, even where the object of study undoubtedly is the instructional system or instruction as a process, authors present their work as if the object is the learning organism. This way of reporting means a loss in accomplishments and progress in instructional theory.

(5) A TTI borrows from other disciplines

Elaboration: A theory can develop only when it defines its jurisdiction and its borders. An instructional theory must absorb results from empirical and theoretical research done outside its boundaries, in other disciplines. But propositions originating from other disciplines must be stated in instructional terms and their sources must be traced and mentioned. Instructional theory should use the results from such diverse fields as human behavior, cognition, computer science, the art of teaching, and media. Researchers in the field of instruction do not themselves study the problems in these fields. They use and translate what their colleagues from other fields have found.

EPILOGUE

If theories are descriptive and if a true theory of instruction must meet the five criteria mentioned, what then is the relationship of instructional theory with Instructional Development, with Cognitive Science, and with the normative theories?

Instructional development or "instructional technology in a broad sense" is a problem-solving methodology. One might say that instructional problems in education and training can be solved in two ways. Problems can be solved in a creative, intuitive way. Or they can be solved in a systematic way. Most practitioners, teachers and designers, solve the daily problems the creative way. Many recommend the systematic approach, which in itself can take many forms, as shown by Gustafson (1981). Does the systematic approach also imply a standpoint about the use of one particular theory or discipline describing the structure and functioning of the instructional system? No, it does not. The systematic approach in itself does not tell the designer what knowledge to look for in the process of solving instructional problems. The approach is eclectic and picks what is suitable. The systematic approach of instructional design is neutral as far as the selection of a specific instructional theory is concerned.

Reigeluth (1983a), among many others, presupposes that knowledge of the learning process is basic to design theories of instruction. The question is to what extent instructional theorists must depend on cognitive science. We believe that a true theory of instruction incorporates and integrates findings from other sciences, including cognitive science. The challenge for research on instruction in this repect is not to copy themes and findings from others but to translate the findings and incorporate them into the theory of instruction. Only then can instruction really profit from the great strides made in cognitive science. Researchers of instruction also have to resist the temptation to study problems lying outside their own field. Researchers tend to do research on the problems where tradition is strongest, the research community is most productive, and prospective results will fit into a strong framework. Up till now, such problems can more easily be found outside the variables of the instructional system than among them. However, a true theory of instruction chooses its own themes and translates findings from other sciences.

Designers of instruction, certainly in the Netherlands, experience a growing sense of identity as an academic community, because of the work of theorists who created models or instructional design theories. Their identity as an academic community can only grow if more attention is given to the description of what is known about the structure and functioning of instructional systems. Designing is regarded by engineers, like Jones (1980), as the initiation of change in man-made things. The designer treats as real that which exists in an imagined future. But before predicting the future, Jones points out, we have to know the present. Therefore we can never know enough about the present, that is about the instructional system as it exists. Up till now authors have written more about how to reach the future than about what the present looks like and how it works. We suppose that in the long run instructional models could be used on an even larger scale by designers if these models can refer to a body of knowledge of a less normative character.

But in what way then is an alleged descriptive (classifying, ordering, explaining, and predicting) theory basis for instructional design theories like the Component Display Theory, the Elaboration Theory of Instruction and John Keller's ARCS model of instruction? And what is the difference or, more importantly, what is the relation between an alleged descriptive theory and prescriptive theories? The difference is that the descriptive theory classifies, orders, explains, and predicts phenomena. The prescriptive theory gives rules to be followed by the designer. The relation between the two is that the former is functioning as a source for the latter. When the descriptive theory has given the direction and strength of the relation between methods and outcomes, the prescriptive theory may prescribe the method to be used to reach certain outcomes.

REFERENCES

Bloom, B.S. (1976). *Human characteristics and school learning.* New York: McGraw-Hill Book Company.

Bloom, B.S. (1981). *All our children learning.* New York: McGraw-Hill Book Company.

Bruner, J.S. (1966). *Toward a theory of instruction.* Cambridge, Mass.: Harvard University Press.

Carroll, J.B. (1963). A model of school learning. *Teachers College Record, 64*(8), 723-733.

Gage, N.L. (1978). *The scientific basis for the art of teaching.* New York: Teachers College Press.

Gagné, R.M. (1976). *The conditions of learning* (3rd ed.). New York: Holt, Rinehart and Winston.

Glaser, R. (1966). The design of instruction. In John I. Goodlad (Ed.), *The changing american school: NSSE 65th Yearbook* (pp. 215-242). Chicago: University of Chicago Press.

Gustafson, K.L. (1981). *Survey of instructional development models.* Syracuse, NY: ERIC Clearinghouse on Information Resources.

Jones, J.C. (1980). *Design methods: Seeds of human futures.* New York: John Wiley and Sons.

KRO (1983). *Spreeuwenwerk: Een film van Tys Tinbergen & Jan Musch.* Hilversum: KRO Uitzending 1983. Productie Twisk/Nisk.

Merrill, M.D. (1968). Instructional design: A new emphasis in teacher training. *Educational Horizons, 47*(1), 9-20.

Reigeluth, C.M. (1983a). Instructional design: What is it and why is it? In C. M. Reigeluth (Ed.), *Instructional-design: Theories and models* (pp. 3-37). Hillsdale, NJ: Lawrence Erlbaum Associates.

Reigeluth, C.M. (Ed.) (1983b). *Instructional-design: Theories and models.* Hillsdale, NJ: Lawrence Erlbaum Associates.

Reigeluth, C.M. (Ed.) (1987). *Instructional theories in action: Lessons illustrating selected theories and models.* Hillsdale, NJ: Lawrence Erlbaum Associates.

Snelbecker, G.E. (1974). *Learning theory, Instructional theory, and psychoeducational design.* Lanham, New York, London: University Press of America.

2

AN INSTRUCTIONAL DESIGN EXPERT SYSTEM

M. David Merrill
Zhongmin Li
Utah State University

ABSTRACT

The purpose of this project was to develop a prototype expert instructional design system[1] which would demonstrate the feasibility of a consultation system which could be used by inexperienced instructional designers to assist in instructional design decision making. Unlike most so called authoring systems this prototype is a consultation system to guide the instructional design process prior to the programming stage rather than assisting with the programming (implementation) activities.

INTRODUCTION

The prototype gathers information from the user/designer and then makes recommendations for each of the following instructional design decisions:
What is the orienting goal of the instruction?
What is the content structure which best corresponds to this goal?
Guidance for elaborating and instantiating this content structure.
What modules are necessary for teaching the content?
What instructional transactions are best for each of these modules?
Guidance for elaborating and instantiating each transaction.

The output of the consultation is an instructional design specification which identifies each of the modules needed, the instructional objectives associated with each module, the instructional function(s) of each module, the instructional transaction(s) necessary to accomplish each function. This design specification provides the skeleton from which instructional materials can be

developed. Future versions of the system will link the instructional design expert to authoring (implementation) capabilities.

The domain of the prototype system is limited to goals involving concept classification with a KINDS TAXONOMY content structure and goals involving procedures for device operation with a PATH ALGORITHM content structure. Only the KINDS TAXONOMY is illustrated in this chapter. Other domain areas have been identified and future implementations of the system will include these areas to make the system a comprehensive consultation system appropriate for most instructional design situations.

The prototype has been implemented using the S.1 expert system shell (Teknowledge Inc.) and runs on a VAX computer. The knowledge base includes in excess of 400 rules. The next phase of the system will port the expert system to a desk top platform (Macintosh computer with NEXPERT expert system shell) with an interactive graphic user interface.

The prototype explored a number of different reasoning procedures including rules based on decision trees and rules based on the accumulation of evidence using certainty factors. Unlike many expert systems which are directed toward a single decision this prototype makes recommendations on a series of decisions and allows the user/designer to confirm each recommendation as the reasoning proceeds. The prototype explored allowing the user/designer to back up and provide different information if a recommendation was not acceptable. The prototype explored the use of nested miniexperts for information where the user/designer may need more assistance. The prototype uses a mixed approach in which frame based and declarative (rule based) programming is combined with procedural programming which controls the reasoning and information gathering process.

COMPONENTS OF AN INSTRUCTIONAL SYSTEM

Instructional systems can be conceptualized in many ways. To facilitate communication the following paragraphs identify and define the components of an instructional system for which the ID Expert provides design guidance. Figure 1 identifies the following components of an instructional system: (1) Goals, knowledge and student attributes (inputs to the design process); (2) content structure; (3) course organization; (4) sequence; (5) modules; (6) content representation; (7) transactions; and (8) strategy.

Content Structure

Content structure is the organization of the subject matter content. A content structure diagram is often included as part of the content representation.

Different content structures are appropriate for different instructional goals. The ID Expert contains a taxonomy of different types of content structure frames and rules for determining which structure(s) are most appropriate for a given goal and audience characteristics. The ID Expert assists the designer in selecting an appropriate content structure for the goals and student audience of the course. The ID Expert also guides the designer in instantiating this

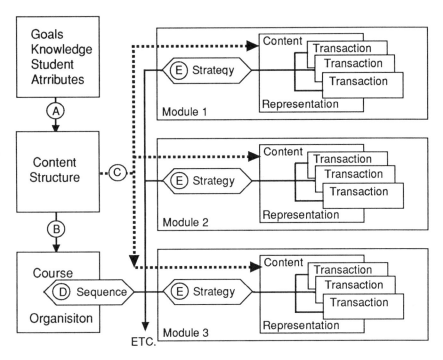

Figure 1. Components of an instructional system.

content structure, that is, the designer is guided in organizing the content previously selected for inclusion in the course. The instantiated content structure is the primary information used by the ID Expert to determine recommended modules, module content, module objectives and course organization.

Module

The module is the primary unit of course organization specified by the ID Expert. A module is a unit of instruction composed of standard components. The figure indicates that a module consists of three primary components:
(1)   a set of transactions which enables the student to interact with the content representation;
(2)   the content representation which is the actual material to be learned or with which the student interacts to learn about the content; and

(3)   a set of strategy rules which determine the next transaction and when the
        student should shift to the next transaction.

Transaction

A transaction is "... a communicative action or activity involving two parties
or two things reciprocally affecting or influencing each other . . ." (Webster).
A transaction is a mutual, dynamic, real-time give-and-take between the
instructional system and the student in which there is an exchange of
information. Many tutorial instructional systems are described in terms of
frames (displays) and questions, however, frames and questions enable only a
limited number of transaction types. Adequate instruction, especially with
experiential subject matter content representation, requires a wider range of
student interaction. A transaction is a complete sequence of presentations and
reactions necessary to accomplish some instructional function. A given
instructional function can often be accomplished by two or more different
types of transactions. The ID Expert includes a taxonomy of transactions
appropriate for particular instructional functions, within particular content
structures for accomplishing particular instructional goals. The ID Expert
recommends appropriate transactions for each function within each module
based on goal characteristics, audience characteristics, the content structure,
and content characteristics.

Strategy

Strategy is a set of rules for determining which transaction should be next and
when the student should shift to the next transaction. Strategy rules also
indicate whether the learner or the system should make this decision.
Recommending strategy rules is beyond the scope of the prototype system.

Content Representation

Content Representation (also called knowledge representation) is the content
material (domain knowledge) with which the student interacts. There are two
major categories of content representation: structural and experiential.
(1)   Structural representations consist of domain knowledge which has been
        selected and isolated for presentation to the student. This information
        often consists of generalities, examples, prerequisite material, context,
        and background material that has been collected about a given domain.
        Structural knowledge is similar to more familiar "text book"
        representations but may include graphic materials such as animations,
        video, and nonexperiential simulations.
(2)   Experiential representations consist of domain knowledge which
        simulate devices, events or processes in a way which enables the student

to interact directly with these materials. Experiential representations respond to student input in ways similar to the response of the actual device, event or process simulated. The ID Expert recommends the content representation(s) necessary to implement the recommended transactions.

Course Organization

The course organization is the network of modules and the possible paths that the student may take in traversing this network. Course organization identifies pre and post integrative modules, menus, instructional modules and paths connecting these organizational components. The ID Expert recommends content organization based on goal characteristics, audience characteristics and the content structure.

Sequence

Sequence is a set of rules for determining which module should be next and when the student should shift to the next module. Sequence rules also indicate whether the learner or the system should make this decision. Sequence rules are beyond the scope of the prototype.

REPRESENTATION

Frames

Much of the knowledge that is included in the ID Expert knowledge base is represented by frames. Frames should not be confused with programmed instruction display-type frames. The frames are knowledge representation frameworks each of which contain "slots" for various specific information. A frame "knows" what information it needs to be completely instantiated and can therefore be used to guide the process of gathering this specific information from the user/designer (knowledge acquisition). Frames, especially transaction frames, may contain within them procedures for conducting a particular interaction with the student. It is unnecessary for the user/designer to reinvent these interactive procedures because knowledge about how to conduct a particular kind of interaction is captured (contained within) the frame representing this transaction. Once the frame has been selected and instantiated with the specific information needed to fill its information slots it knows what to do to interact with the student. The design process consists of selecting the appropriate frame for a given situation, goal or student.

The types of frames included in the ID Expert include frames for the various types of content structures and their internal relationships, the various types of course organization and their internal relationships, the various types of strategies and their internal relationships, and the various types of transactions and their internal relationships. Having selected a particular content structure, course organization, strategy or transaction a considerable amount of knowledge is already specified and it is not necessary for the user/designer to reinvent this imbedded knowledge. The rules of the system enable the user/designer to make selections among the various available frames to select those which are most appropriate for a given situation. Having made this selection many other decisions have already been made as they are incorporated in the various frames.

In the following sections we have conceptually described a content structure frame and a transaction frame.

Content structure frame
In this brief report we have illustrated the system as it guides the design of concept lessons. One of the content structures recommended by the system is a kinds-of taxonomy. Figure 2 illustrates the basic structure of a kinds taxonomy. This "kinds" frame knows that there must be a superordinate concept identified and thus queries the user/designer for the name of this superordinate concept. This frame also knows that there are two or more coordinate concepts and queries the user/designer for the number and names of each of the coordinate concepts. This frame also knows that each of the coordinate concepts can also act as a superordinate concept with subordinate coordinate concepts. Hence the user/designer is queried about subordinate concepts until he/she indicates that the taxonomy has been sufficiently elaborated.

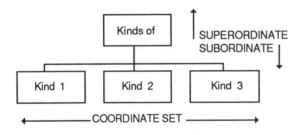

Figure 2. Illustration of KINDS taxonomy.

The kinds taxonomy frame also has slots for additional information. Most important is the relationship between the coordinate concepts at any level and the focus of the instruction in relation to any set of coordinate concepts.

The relationship among coordinate concepts can be independent, coordinate, ordered, overlapped or on a continuum. INDEPENDENT concepts means that the concepts in a coordinate set are discrete categories that are not likely to be confused with each other. COORDINATE concepts means that the concepts in a coordinate set are likely to be confused with one another. ORDERED concepts means that the concepts in the coordinate set are not only likely to be confused with one another but that the categories themselves can be ordered on some dimension such as size, age, importance, etc. OVERLAPPED concepts means that the concepts in the coordinate set do not have nice clean borders with neighbouring concepts. Some examples may be hard to classify as to membership in one concept or the other because boundaries of the categories overlap. CONTINUUM concepts means that the boundaries between the concepts in the coordinate set are ill defined or that there are no boundaries between the various categories. The instances can be ordered along some dimension but any lines between categories are arbitrary or not easily defined. The kinds taxonomy frame queries the user/designer to find the nature of this coordinate set relationship. This information is used by decision rules for selecting course organization and transactions.

The focus of the instruction with regard to a given set of coordinate concepts can be identify, discriminate, rank, generalize or kinds. IDENTIFY focus means that the primary goal of the instruction is to have students identify items as examples or nonexamples of a single concept without regard for the other concepts in the coordinate set. DISCRIMINATE focus means that the primary goal of the instruction is to have students discriminate instances of the various concept categories in the coordinate set from one another. RANK focus means that the primary goal of the instruction is to have students rank instances of a superordinate concept along some dimension represented by coordinate concepts. A ranking focus is more appropriate than a discriminate focus when the coordinate concepts are ordered or form a continuum. GENERALIZE focus means that the primary goal of the instruction is to have students identify members of two or more coordinate concepts as members of a more general superordinate concept. KINDS of focus means that the primary goal of the instruction is to have students identify instances of a subordinate concept as instances of a superordinate concept without regard for other concepts in the coordinate set. The kinds taxonomy frame also queries the user or infers the focus of the instruction from other information provided by the user.

The kinds taxonomy frame also gathers information on other attributes of the coordinate concepts but these details are not described here.

This description of a kinds taxonomy content structure frame should help you see the nature of a frame. It is not necessary for the user of the ID Expert to

construct or remember all of the information about concepts contained in the kinds taxonomy frame. The frame representation contains slots for all this information and the system queries the user for the information which it needs to instantiate all of these slots. When the user has provided the necessary specific information the ID Expert can use this information to provide the user with a diagram of the content structure and its characteristics as well as using the information contained within this frame to make decisions about course organization, sequence, strategy and transactions.

Transaction frame

Transaction frames contain slots for the content information necessary to provide a particular kind of interaction with the student. These frames already contain algorithms for conducting this transaction and it is unnecessary for the user/designer to reconstruct each of these interactions. The system queries the user/designer about the specific information necessary to instantiate the slots in the frame. Once this information has been provided the transaction frame is ready to interact with the student.

Figures 3, 4 and 5 illustrate a "Compare" transaction which might be a transaction appropriate for teaching discrimination of coordinate concepts. This particular illustration has been instantiated for learner control. The transaction allows the learner to select values on the critical attributes of the concept being taught (in the illustration various kinds of pumps). The user can then select an example illustrating these attributes (Figure 4). The learner can then select a second example with these same attributes to compare with the first example (Figure 5). The learner can repeat this process with a number of examples limited only by the number of examples with which the transaction frame is instantiated. The user can also return to the attribute table and select a new set of attribute values. This transaction is often combined with a contrast transaction (not illustrated here) which enables the user to contrast examples each with different attribute values.

The compare transaction frame knows the information needed to instantiate its specific information slots. The user/designer is asked to list the attributes of the concept and the values these attributes can assume. The user is asked to supply a set of illustrations illustrating the concept and to indicate for each example the attribute values illustrated. This is the minimal instantiation required by the compare transaction frame.

This transaction frame also contains a number of other parameters which enable the user/designer to customize this transaction to the situation. Often the decision rules in the expert system make recommendations on the values for these parameters. Some of these parameters include: *learner control*, does the system or the user select attribute values; *pacing*, does the system or the

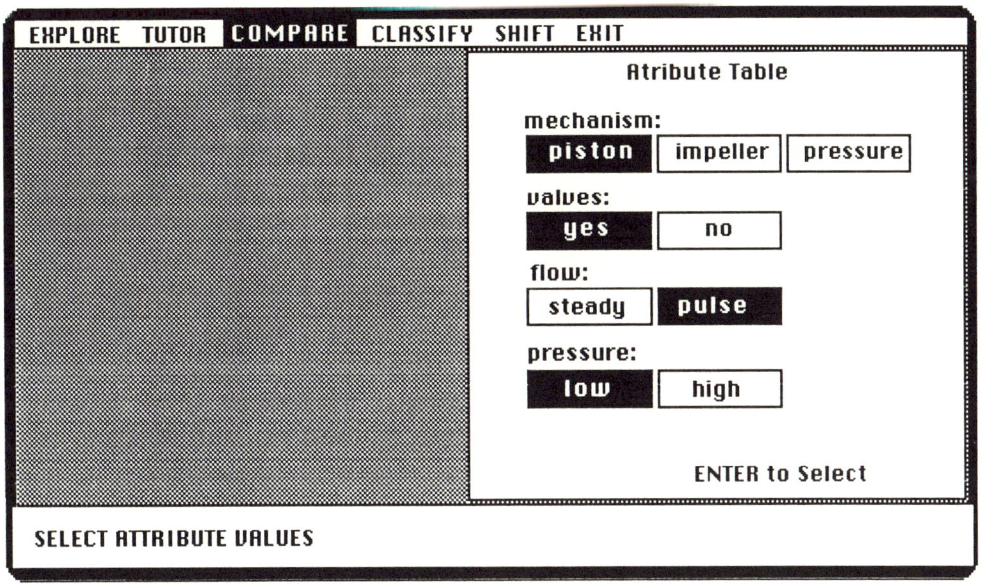

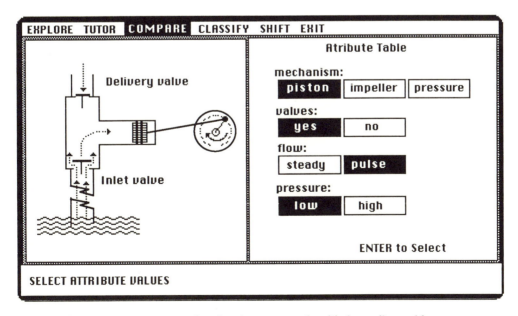

Figure 3. Compare contrast transaction showing attribute table.

Figure 4. Compare contrast transaction showing an example with the attribute table.

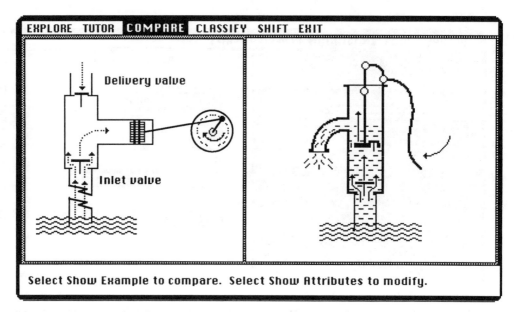

Figure 5. Compare contrast transaction showing a comparison example.

user decide when to present an example and for how long; *type of illustration*, options include static computer graphic (such as those shown), animated computer graphic, video disc (still, motion, with audio). These represent some of the parameters. There are a number of others not described here.

The compare transaction represents only 1 of 12 possible transactions currently included in the concept portion of the ID Expert system. Ultimately the ID Expert will include a large library of transaction frames appropriate for a wide variety of instructional transactions. The VAX version of the system does not yet include facilities for instantiating transaction frames but the Macintosh version currently being constructed will include this capability.

Rules

In addition to frames the instructional design knowledge contained in the ID Expert system consists of IF - THEN rules. These rules contain the knowledge about which frame is appropriate for a given instructional design decision. These sets of rules guide the selection of content structure given goals, student characteristics and situational constraints; the selection of course organization and strategy given the instantiated content structure plus the information on goals, students and the situation; the selection of module strategy and transactions given information about course organization, goals, students and situation.

These rules can be specified by decision trees, decision tables and certainty factors but are represented in the system in a similar format. We have not presented any of the formal rules in this chapter but will attempt to show you the nature of the decisions involved in a couple of these rule sets.

Content structure selection rules
In the current system content structure is selected as a function of orientation of the instruction (What is it? How do you do it? Why does it work?); the nature of the object(s) of instruction (symbols, devices, events or persons); whether a specific object or class (general) of objects is involved; and the particular focus of instruction (discriminate, sort, generalize or rank). Depending on the particular path in the decision tree other attributes are sometimes required to make decisions. A partitial decision path is illustrated by Figure 6. Each terminal node is indicated as a Kind Taxonomy which calls the Kind Taxonomy frame and proceeds to query the user/designer for the information necessary to instantiate this frame.

The ID Expert queries the user/designer for information needed to make a recommendation about content structure. In the actual implementation of the system there is an information gathering section at the front where most of the information needed by the various decision rules is gathered.

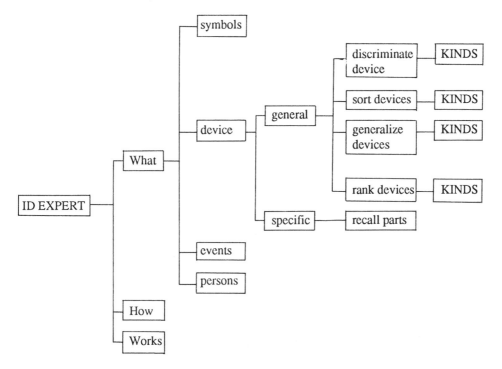

Figure 6. Decision rule for selecting KINDS taxonomy content structure.

Transaction selection rules

Many of the rules in the KINDS consultation involve rules based on the accumulation of evidence using certainty factors. These rules are specified by a table of certainty factors for each value of each attribute for each conclusion.

We will illustrate reasoning by the accumulation of evidence as implemented for selecting transaction frames for concept instruction (kinds taxonomy content structure). The selection of transaction type depends on a large number of attributes indicated by the following function:

Transaction.Type =   F(Module.Function, Concept. Relationships, Concept. Focus, Concept. Characteristics (Embedded, Concrete, Number of attributes, Text), Student (Motivation, Familiarity, Locus of Control)).

Each of these attributes can have up to 8 values. A decision tree based on 10 attributes with from 3 to 7 values for each attribute would result in over 800,000 branches if specified by a decision tree. Specifying all the possibilities for such a decision tree would be a very difficult task. The accumulation of evidence is a more practical method for specifying such complex combinations of rules.

When reasoning by the accumulation of evidence each possible recommendation is given a certainty factor which indicates that if this were the only piece of information known what would be the certainty of a particular recommendation. Certainty factors vary from -1.0 to + 1.0. A -1.0 means that for this value never recommend the associated conclusion. A + 1.0 means that for this value always recommend the associated conclusion. Values less than 1.0 and greater than -1.0 are combined via a mathematical relationship as each rule fires. Thus until a value of -1.0 or +1.0 is attained every conclusion is still possible after the given rule fires. When the next rules fires the certainty factor associated with each conclusion is either increased (if the value for the new rule is greater than the value currently associated with the conclusion) or decreased (if the value for the new rule is less than the value currently associated with the conclusion) until all the rules have fired. At this point another rule indicates that all conclusions exceeding some cutoff value should be displayed to the user/designer. This means that more than one conclusion (in this case transaction type) may be recommended for a particular function of a particular module.

A portion of the Transaction.Type certainty factor table is shown in Table 1. The particular attributes and values listed have not all been described in this

Table 1
Transaction Type

TRANSACTION TYPE = F(FUNCTION, RELATIONSHIPS, CHARACTERISTICS, STUDENTS, FOCUS)

IF FUNCTION = THEN TRANSACTION TYPE =

	SYNT	SUM	EXPO	CNVT	CMCN	EDIT	INTR	SORT	LABL	RANK	QUES
Overview	0.40	0.30	0.10	0.20	0.00	-1.00	-1.00	-1.00	-1.00	-1.00	0.10
Presentation new	-1.00	-1.00	-0.40	0.40	0.40	0.00	0.00	0.00	0.00	0.00	0.20
Remediation (old)	0.30	0.30	0.20	0.40	0.40	0.30	0.30	0.30	0.30	0.30	0.30
Practice (early)	-1.00	-1.00	-1.00	-1.00	0.00	0.40	0.40	0.40	0.40	0.40	0.30
Practice (late)	-1.00	-1.00	-1.00	-1.00	0.40	0.40	0.40	0.40	0.40	0.40	0.30
Review	0.40	0.40	0.40	0.40	0.10	0.00	0.00	0.00	0.00	0.00	0.10
Assess/diag	-1.00	-1.00	-1.00	-1.00	-1.00	0.40	0.40	0.40	0.40	0.40	0.30

IF CONCEPT RELATIONSHIPS =

	SYNT	SUM	EXPO	CNVT	CMCN	EDIT	INTR	SORT	LABL	RANK	QUES
Independent	-1.00	0.10	0.00	0.00	-0.20	0.00	0.00	0.00	0.20	-1.00	0.20
Coordinate set	0.10	0.00	0.00	0.00	0.20	0.20	0.20	0.20	0.10	-1.00	0.20
Order	0.10	0.00	0.00	0.00	0.10	0.10	0.10	0.00	0.10	0.30	0.00
Overlap	0.10	0.00	0.00	0.00	0.00	0.10	0.10	0.00	0.00	0.30	0.00
Continuum	0.10	0.00	0.00	0.00	0.00	0.00	0.00	-1.00	-1.00	0.30	0.00
Unknown	0.00	0.00	0.00	0.00	0.00	0.00	0.00	0.00	0.00	0.00	0.00

KEY

Transaction Type	Abbreviation
Synthesis	SYNT
Summary	SUM
Exposition	EXPO
Conversational Tutorial	CNVT
Compare and Contrast	CMCN
Edit	EDIT

Transaction Type	Abbreviation
Interpret	INTR
Sort	SORT
Label	LABL
Rank	RANK
Question	QUES

paper but you should not be concerned with the particular attributes but only with the form of this type of reasoning.

Certainty factors can be determined from a variety of sources. The first is the experience of the domain Expert (M. David Merrill in this case). A given attribute is considered and its relative contribution to the various conclusions is indicated. A certainty value reflecting this relative contribution is then assigned to each cell in the table representing the contribution of that value of the attribute to the conclusion in the column. Other sources of certainty factors are empirical findings where the values of the attribute may have been independent variables in an experimental study and the conclusion the dependent variable. Various schemes are used for combining certainty factors. The scheme which is part of the inference engine of the S.1 expert system shell combines certainty factors in such a way that when a large number of attributes are included the values must be lower than when only a few attributes are included. The actual values were empirically adjusted until the certainty values assigned to the conclusions reflected the relative weight that the domain expert would give to a particular conclusion.

ORGANIZATION OF THE SYSTEM

ID EXPERT is a consultation system which gathers necessary information from the user/designer and then makes instructional design recommendations to the user. The following outline provides a summary of this consultation process. QUERY means to ask the user/designer a series of questions concerning the audience and the goal of the instruction. RECOMMEND implies that the system uses the information provided to do some reasoning and then makes a recommendation to the user/designer as a result of this reasoning. INSTANTIATE/ELABORATE is a knowledge acquisition function which gathers information specific to the user/designers instructional task in order to make recommendations specific to this content material.

The prototype has three distinct parts: the goal consultation, the kinds consultation and the path consultation. As a result of the goal consultation the system recommends a goal and content structure to the user. The system then assists the user to instantiate and elaborate the recommended content structure in terms of the specific content to be taught. The prototype can reason about only two types of content structure: the kinds and path content structures. Only the kinds content structure is illustrated in this chapter.

The following outlines the major parts of the consultation system:

GOAL CONSULTATION
        QUERY: Title

QUERY: Audience Attributes
QUERY: Goal Attributes
RECOMMEND/QUERY: Goal
QUERY: Goal Clarification
RECOMMEND: Content Structure
KINDS CONSULTATION
QUERY: Content Attributes
INSTANTIATE/ELABORATE: Kinds Content Structure
RECOMMEND: Course Organization
RECOMMEND: Module Functions
RECOMMEND: Transaction Types
RECOMMEND: Transaction Characteristics
DISPLAY: ID Specification for course

SAMPLE DIALOGUES

Because of the S.1 implementation of the current prototype the interaction with the system is very linear as reflected in the following consultations with the system. Future implementations of the system will provide a more interactive graphic interface with the user. The prototype concentrates on making reasonable decisions. The report of these decisions is textual.

The following are edited typescripts of actual interactions with the system. The order of some queries have been changed for clarity. The typescripts have been divided into sections which correspond to the organization of the system. These titles (shown in bold) do not appear in the actual typescript. User/designer input is shown by >. Comments which are not part of the typescript are shown in italics inside curly brackets { *comment here* }.

KINDS CONSULTATION

QUERY: Title

1: What is the title of the course?
1> PUMPS

QUERY: Audience Attributes

2: What is the locus of control of this group of students?
Type HELP for more information.
{*Many items are accompanied by more detailed information . Typing HELP displays this information. HELP is illustrated here but omitted from the remainder of the typescript for clarity.*}

2>   HELP
       Locus of Control is a variable which refers to the amount of
       control a student feels that they have in a situation. When
       students feel that they are in control they are willing to make
       decisions and to direct their own activities. When students feel
       that others are in control they are more willing to let others direct
       them and make decisions for them. If you have data on the
       general orientation of the students either from formal tests of
       locus of control or from observing the students this information
       is helpful in making instructional decisions. If the students are
       managers, supervisors or other leaders their orientation is likely
       to be INTERNAL. If the students are not in a leadership position
       then their orientation is often EXTERNAL.

       EXTERNAL locus of control means that the students generally
       feel that others are in control.

       INTERNAL locus of control means that the students generally
       feel that they are in control.
2>   UNKNOWN
       { *It is legal to answer any question with UNKNOWN if the
       user/designer does not have the information requested.* }

3:     What is the average motivation for this group of students?
       Type HELP for more information.
3>   UNKNOWN
       { *Motivation contains a nested expert. The user could have typed
       HIGH, MODERATE or LOW and continued with the
       consultation. By typing UNKNOWN the nested motivation expert
       is called and more detailed questions enable the system to
       recommend the level of motivation.* }

4:     Why will the student take this instruction?
       Volunteer - students will have chosen to take this instruction.
       Required - students will be required to take this instruction.
4>   REQUIRED

5:     Will this instruction contribute to a job promotion for the
       student?
5>   YES

6:     Will this instruction enable or require a job change for the
       student?
6>   YES

7:    Did the student request the job change which requires this instruction?

7>   YES

8:    Did the student request the job change which requires this instruction?

8>   REQUESTED

INTERMEDIATE RESULT:
It has been determined that the student's motivation is high.

9:    Will the student use the acquired skill primarily as:
      CONSUMER - who needs general information.
      SUPERVISOR - who directs the technical work of others.
      TECHNICIAN - who executes skills to perform a service, produce a product or make repairs.
      PROBLEM SOLVER - who understands how a device or process works in order to predict outcomes, derive new rules or procedures or design new products or communications.

9>   TECHNICIAN

QUERY: Goal Attributes

10:   Which of the following best describes what the student will learn?
      WHAT.IS - What it is?
      HOW.TO - How to do it?
      WORKS - How does it work?

10>   WHAT.IS

11:   The student will be expected to demonstrate the acquired skill with:
      SYMBOLS - including language, numbers or other symbols.
      DEVICES - including devices or equipment.
      EVENTS - including processes or procedures.
      PERSONS - including personal characteristics or rules.

11>   DEVICES

12:   Will the student be expected to demonstrate the acquired skill with:
      SPECIFIC - a specific object or set of objects which is the same from one occasion to the next?

GENERAL - sets of different objects which differ from one
occasion to the next?

12>   GENERAL

13:   How familiar are the students with the content of the instruction
(HIGH, MODERATE, LOW)?

13>   LOW

14:   What is the required level of mastery (HIGH, MODERATE,
LOW)?

14>   HIGH

RECOMMEND/QUERY: Goal

15:   Which is an appropriate orienting goal for your instruction?
DISCRIMINATE - The student will be able to discriminate two
or more different kinds of objects, devices or equipment.
SORT - The student will be able to sort objects, devices or
equipment into categories.
GENERALIZE - The student will be able to identify different
objects, devices or equipment as instances of a more general
category.
ORDER - The student will be able to order a series of objects,
devices or equipment relative to some dimension.

15>   DISCRIMINATE

RECOMMEND: Content Structure

INTERMEDIATE RESULT:
A KINDS TAXONOMY Content Structure is recommended.

INSTANTIATE/ELABORATE: Kinds Content Structure

Now, we are building the kinds taxonomy from the top of the tree:

16:   What is the top node concept?
16>   Pumps

17:   Do you wish to expand on pumps?
17>   YES

18:   What is the relationship between the categories in the coordinate
set for pumps (INDEPENDENT, COORDINATE, ORDERED,
OVERLAP, CONTINUUM)?

{ If the user answers UNKNOWN here a more detailed set of questions are asked to assist in the determination of the relationship between the members of the coordinate set. }

18> COORDINATE

19: List the kinds of Pumps in this coordinate set.
19> piston, centrifugal, jet

20: What is the primary focus of the instruction (IDENTIFY, DISCRIMINATE, RANK, GENERALIZE, KINDS.OF, PLACE. HOLDER)?
Type HELP for more information.
20> DISCRIMINATE
{ While not illustrated by this typescript it is possible that there is an inconsistency between the concept relationship and the focus. If so a message identifying this potential conflict and the alternative courses of action available to the user is presented. The user is allowed to accept the information already provided or to change either the focus or the relationship. }

QUERY: Content Characteristics

22: Are the concepts in the coordinate set EMBEDDED or ISOLATED?
Type HELP for more information.
22> ISOLATED

{ Additional attributes of the individual concepts are acquired at this point but are not included in this edited transcript. }

{ At this point in the dialogue each of the coordinate concepts are taken in turn and the queries for instantiation and content characteristics are repeated until the user/designer indicates that there are no further elaborations. }

27: Do you wish to expand on piston pumps?
27> YES

28: What is the relationship between the concepts in the coordinate set for piston pumps (INDEPENDENT, COORDINATE, ORDERED, OVERLAP, CONTINUUM)?
28> INDEPENDENT

{ ETC. for queries 29 through 44 in the current typescript. }

INTERMEDIATE RESULT
The KINDS content structure for Pumps is as follows:

Pumps
    Piston
        Piston1
        Vane
        Lift
        Diaphragm
Centrifugal
Jet

RECOMMEND: Course Organization

INTERMEDIATE RESULT
The following modules are recommended to teach pumps.

An integrative module for Pumps.

A coordinate set module for Piston, Centrifugal, Jet.
    OBJECTIVE: The student will be able to discriminate instances
of Piston, Centrifugal and Jet Pumps from one another.

A coordinate set module for Piston1, Vane, Lift and Diaphragm Piston
    Pumps.
    OBJECTIVE: The student will be able to discriminate instances
of Piston1, Vane, Lift and Diaphragm Piston Pumps from one
another.

The following course organization is recommended.

Map #1

    A preintegrative module for Pumps

    A menu for the following module(s)
        1. Piston, Centrifugal, Jet Pumps

    A menu for the following module(s)
        2. Piston1 Piston Pumps
        3. Vane Piston Pumps
        4. Lift Piston Pumps
        5. Diaphragm Piston Pumps

A postintegrative module for Pumps

{ *A more complex course organization would have maps within menus and a nested content structure for each of these maps.* }

RECOMMEND: Module Functions

INTERMEDIATE RESULT
Recommended function(s) for preintegrative module Pumps.

A(n) overview function is strongly suggested (cf = .8).

45: What is/are the function(s) of this module?
45> OVERVIEW

{ *In many cases there may be several possible functions for a module in which case the user could select one or several functions for the module.* }

Recommended function(s) for postintegrative module Pumps.

A(n) assessment.diagnosis function is strongly suggested (cf = .8).
A(n) review is weakly suggested (cf = .3).

46: What is/are the function(s) of this module?
46> ASSESSMENT.DIAGNOSIS

Recommended functions(s) for instructional module Piston, Centrifugal, Jet Pumps.

A(n) new presentation function is strongly suggested (cf = .8).
A(n) early practice function is suggested (cf = .75).
A(n) late practice function is suggested (cf = .72).
A(n) assessment.diagnosis function is suggested (cf = .64).

47: What is/are the function(s) of this module?
47> NEW.PRESENTATION, EARLY.PRACTICE, LATE.PRACTICE

{ *This dialogue continues for each of the modules identified for the course structure until all the functions have been recommended and accepted by the user/designer.* }

RECOMMEND: Transaction Types and Characteristics

INTERMEDIATE RESULT
Recommended transaction type(s) for preintegrative module Pumps
  overview function.

  A(n) summary transaction is suggested (cf = .48).
  A(n) synthesis transaction is suggested (cf = .44).

49:   Which transaction(s) would you prefer?
49> SYNTHESIS

Recommended   transaction   characteristics   for   a(n)   synthesis
  transaction.

  Presentation sequence should be sequential.
  Presentation mode should be inquisitory.
  Transaction control should be learner control.
  Required content representation(s) should include:
      taxonomy
      definition
      examples
  Optional content representations(s) should include:
      attribute.definition
      attribute.isolation

Recommended transaction type(s) for postintegrative module Pumps
  assessment/diagnosis function.

  Since the content is not integrated there is no need to integrate
  the assessment. Combining assessment from each module within
  the course organization map makes up the heterogeneous test for
  the postintegrative module.

Recommended transaction type(s) assessment function for the
  instructional module Piston, Centrifugal, Jet Pumps.

  A(n) sort transaction is suggested (cf = .73).
  A(n) label transaction is suggested (cf = .62).
  A(n) interpret transaction is suggested (cf = .52).

50:   Which transaction(s) would you prefer?
50> SORT

Recommended transaction characteristics for a(n) sort transaction.

> Presentation sequence should be sequential.
> Presentation mode should be inquisitory.
> Transaction control should be learner control.
> Required content representation(s) should include:
>   examples
> Optional content representations(s) should include:
>   definition
>   attribute.isolation

{ *The consultation continues to make recommendations for each function of each module. The user/designer confirms the recommendations by selecting transactions from the options presented until all of the modules, functions and transactions have been specified.* }

DISPLAY: ID Specification for course

{ *At this point a complete specification for the course is presented by the system. This is a compilation of all the intermediate results formated. This presentation has been omitted here because of space limitations.* }

FUTURE

We are currently in phase 3 of the Instructional Design Expert System Project. In the current phase the system is being converted to a desk top platform using the NEXPERT expert system shell on a Macintosh computer. The Macintosh version will include frames for transactions and the guidance for the user/designer to instantiate these transaction shells. The Macintosh version will also use a more visual graphic interface where the content structure, course organization, module strategy and transactions will be presented in graphic form rather than in only text. Information gathering will also involve a graphic user interface rather than single questions presented in a linear format.

Future phases of the project call for significantly increasing the scope of the system to a wide range of potential instructional outcomes. The scope will also be increased to take into account a wider range of user and situational variables. In addition the expert system will be designed so that it can interface with a variety of authoring systems so that the result of the design effort will be actual instruction ready to deliver to a student population.

Note

1. Developed for the Army Research Institute for the Behavioral and Social Science, Alexandria, Virginia in cooperation with Human Technology Inc., McLean, Virginia and the U.S. Office of Training and Development Training Assistance Branch.

REFERENCES

Hayes-Roth, R., Waterman, D.A., & Lenat, D.B. (Eds.) (1983). *Building expert systems.* Reading, MA: Addison-Wesley Publishing Company, Inc.

Li, Z. (1988). *IDS: An instructional design expert system.* Dissertation, Los Angeles, CA: University of Southern California.

Merrill, M.D. (1987). The new component design theory: Instructional design for courseware authoring. *Instructional Science, 14*(1), 1-10.

Merrill, M.D. (1987). An expert system for instructional design. *IEEE Expert, 2*(2), 25-37.

Merrill, M.D. (1986). Prescriptions for an authoring system. *Journal of Computer-Based Instruction, 12*(4), 90-96.

Merrill, M.D. (1983). The component display theory. In C.M. Reigeluth (Ed.), *Instructional-design theories and models: An overview of their current status* (pp. 279-333). Hillsdale: NJ: Lawrence Erlbaum Associates, Publishers.

Merrill, M.D., & Li, Z. (1988). *Implementation of an expert system for instructional design: Phase Two.* McLean, VA: Human Technology, Inc.

Teknowledge, Inc. (1986). *S.1 Reference Manual*, version 2.2. Palo Alto, CA: Author.

Waterman, D.A. (1985). *A guide to expert systems.* Reading, MA: Addison-Wesley Publishing Company, Inc.

3

THE "COMPLETION STRATEGY" IN PROGRAMMING INSTRUCTION: THEORETICAL AND EMPIRICAL SUPPORT

Jeroen J.G. van Merriënboer
Hein P.M. Krammer
University of Twente

ABSTRACT

The completion strategy is an instructional strategy for the teaching of introductory programming that heavily emphasizes the modification and extension of existing, well-designed and working programs. Thus, in contrast to more traditional instructional strategies, it does not emphasize the design and coding of complete, new programs. The goal of this article is to offer theoretical and empirical support to the effectiveness of the completion strategy. First, a theoretical framework is sketched that relates general instructional strategies for introductory programming courses to well-known instructional tactics. As it turns out, most of these tactics can be easily implemented in the completion strategy. Second, data from experiments on cognitive style, group work, and instructional methods are presented that give support to the effectiveness of the completion strategy and its superiority over other strategies. Finally, the results of those studies are discussed and related to our theoretical framework.

INTRODUCTION

Nowadays, many high schools offer their students the possibility to attend introductory programming courses. One of the most often cited rationales for such courses is that learning computer programming will improve students' higher level cognitive skills, that is, general problem solving skills that are also of value in other domains. However, there is yet little empirical evidence regarding transfer of such skills from computer programming to other domains.

Moreover, most introductory programming courses labor under difficulties because of the students' low level of performance and disappointing learning outcomes with respect to more direct goals, such as acquiring knowledge of basic commands and gaining some skill in the comprehension and generation of programs (e.g., Dalbey & Linn, 1985; Kurland, Pea, Clement, & Mawby, 1986; Linn, 1985; Linn, Sloane, & Clancey, 1987; Pea & Kurland, 1984; Perkins, Hancock, Hobbs, Martin, & Simmons, 1986; Pintrich, Berger, & Stemmer, 1987). In fact, these low learning outcomes may well account for the lack of transfer because the cognitive skills that are expected to develop out of programming no doubt depend upon attaining programming skills to a reasonable degree.

Several suggestions have been made to increase the effectiveness of introductory programming courses, and thus the possibility of transfer to other domains. One interesting suggestion is to devote more time to the reading, comprehension, completion, amplification and modification of existing programs (e.g., Dalbey, Tourniaire, & Linn, 1985; Deimel & Moffat, 1982; Pea, 1986). In this article, we will refer to this approach as the completion strategy (Note 1). The purpose of this paper is to report about our theoretical and experimental studies that support the effectiveness of the completion strategy.

The paper is structured as follows. First, the theoretical basis of the research is explained. Three instructional strategies are discussed and related to six well-known instructional tactics. In this analysis, the completion strategy is found to be best compatible with all instructional tactics. Second, three experimental studies are reviewed that give support to the usefulness of the completion strategy. Finally, the results of those studies are related to our theoretical framework.

THEORETICAL FOUNDATION OF THE COMPLETION STRATEGY

In a theoretical article (Van Merriënboer & Krammer, 1987), the authors identified from the educational field three prevailing strategies for teaching introductory programming. In addition, six tactics were derived from cognitive theory and relevant research. These tactics should be used for the design of introductory programming courses; they relate to concrete computer models, programming plans, design diagrams, worked examples, basic skills, and task variation. The idea is that the instructional strategy in which all six desirable tactics can be most easily implemented is superior to other strategies. In the following sections, the strategies, tactics and evaluations of strategies will be briefly reviewed.

Instructional strategies for programming instruction

Instructional strategies are general plans for designing instruction that pursue high-level goals, or course objectives, that teachers consider desirable. For introductory programming, these goals at least include the gaining of some factual knowledge about basic commands and syntax of the language, the understanding of the semantics of the language to be able to comprehend programs, and the development of skill in the generation of programs. Three general strategies may be distinguished to reach these goals.

Two of these strategies emphasize that the students should immediately start off with designing and/or coding programs, that is, program generation. The first "generation strategy" is heavily inspired by the discipline of structured programming. An important feature of this approach is its emphasis on both algorithm and program design in a systematic top-down fashion. Students receive from the outset of the course problems for which algorithms have to be developed. They are urged to work according to a model of stepwise refinement that should allow the students to concentrate on the semantic content of the algorithm because less attention is required to plan and execute actions on lower program code levels.

The second "generation strategy" is closely related to the "spiral approach" (Shneiderman, 1977) for teaching introductory programming courses. An important feature of this approach is its emphasis on stepwise incremental learning, so that complex ideas are always built from combinations of simpler ideas. Each step contains both syntactic and semantic elements, presents a minimal extension of previous knowledge, is explained in relation to already acquired knowledge, and is trained in exercises. Consequently, the students receive in the beginning of the course trivial problems that emphasize syntactic and lower level semantic knowledge; during the course, the problems gradually become more complex in the coding as well as the design aspects that they require.

The completion strategy is the only strategy that emphasizes the reading, modification and extension of existing, well-designed and working programs. For this reason, students are confronted with non-trivial design problems from the beginning of the course, but these problems are always presented in combination with their complete or partial solutions in the form of well-designed and well-documented (partial) programs. The students' tasks gradually become more complex during the course, changing from using, reading and tracing programs, through modifying and completing programs, to independently designing and coding new programs or subprograms.

Instructional tactics for programming instruction

In contrast to instructional strategies, instructional tactics are specific design plans that prescribe methods to reach desired learning outcomes under given circumstances. Two types of instructional tactics can be distinguished. Tactics for declarative instruction include methods for the initial presentation of information about the computer, the programming language and the design process to facilitate the storage of new, factual knowledge; tactics for procedural instruction include methods for the design of practice to facilitate the development of -procedural- programming skills.

Tactics for declarative instruction

A first tactic implies that students must learn a simplified computer model early in instruction. According to DuBoulay (1986; see also Duboulay, O'Shea, & Monk, 1981), the presentation of a concrete computer model is useful to facilitate the instruction of programming concepts like assignment statements. Mayer (1975) expects computer models to work as advance organizers. Indeed, his research (Mayer, 1976; Mayer & Bromage, 1980) confirmed the effectiveness of computer model instruction.

A second tactic stresses the importance of directly teaching programming plans or cliches of programming code (Ehrlich & Soloway, 1984; Soloway, 1985). Studies of the differences in program comprehension by experts and novices suggest that experts organize their knowledge of programs into cognitive structures that contain templates of language code, which are associated with specific programming problems (Adelson, 1981; Atwood, Turner, Ramsey, Hooper, & Sidorsky, 1977; Barfield, 1986; McKeithen, Reitman, Rueter, & Hirtle, 1981; Shneiderman, 1976, 1977; Weiser & Shertz, 1983). The development of such cognitive structures can be facilitated by the explicit teaching of programming plans: Templates of programming code in combination with comments that describe the goals and reasons for the various expressions in the template.

A last tactic for declarative instruction concerns the presentation of design diagrams. Expert programmers have the disposal of a general design schema, that is, abstract knowledge concerning the processes involved in generating a good design and its overall structure. Jeffries, Turner, Polson & Atwood (1981) distinguished three major mechanisms: Decomposition of the problem into modules, specification of the relationships among modules, and specification of data structures. Novices, on the other hand, do not possess a general design schema and usually have severe difficulties in coordinating their activities. Instructional materials may support systematic design by explicitly presenting a design diagram; for example, a flow chart which prescribes in detail the actions and methods that ensure a systematic and effective design process.

Tactics for procedural instruction

A first tactic for procedural instruction is related to the use of worked examples. Anderson, Farrell & Sauers (1984) reported that students who start practicing - after they have learned new programming concepts - rely heavily on concrete examples of problem solutions related to the problem at hand. These examples function as analogies that students use as blue-prints to map their new solutions and to bridge the gap between acquired, factual knowledge and desired programming behavior. According to Anderson, Boyle, Corbett & Lewis (1986), the worked examples should also be annotated with information about what they are supposed to illustrate.

A second tactic stresses the importance of extensive training of basic cognitive skills. Students may have difficulties with higher skills involved in programming because the necessary basic skills (such as applying syntactic rules and proceeding in the programming environment by using the editor, interpreter or compiler, and debugging aids) have not been sufficiently practiced (e.g., Resnick & Ford, 1981). By extensive training of such low-level skills students' processing efficiency is increased so that the cognitive system is able to simultaneously perform other, higher-order tasks that do make demands on working memory, such as reformulating the problem or designing algorithms.

A final tactic for procedural instruction is related to the degree of variation in assigned tasks. The knowledge base of an expert programmer is estimated to include ten to hundreds of thousands of highly task-specific procedures (Brooks, 1977). Moreover, it takes at least 100 hours to achieve only modest facility in programming skill and several years of practice to become an expert programmer. An instructional implication is that there must be enough variation in practice to develop a knowledge base that is broad enough to handle a variety of problems. Even in introductory programming courses, some variation should be offered by the assignment of different tasks and the presentation of a broad range of both programming problems and solutions to those problems.

An evaluation of instructional strategies

Three instructional tactics can be easily implemented in generation strategies as well as the completion strategy. These non-discriminating tactics include the presentation of concrete computer models, the use of design diagrams, and the extensive training of basic skills. Other tactics are, according to our view, more easily implemented in the completion strategy.

First, the presentation of worked examples takes place in a simple and natural manner in the completion strategy because there is a direct bond between examples (that usually have the form of partial programs) and practice. The students have to study the examples carefully because they cannot correctly finish an assignment to modify or extend the program without studying it. As an extra benefit, the worked examples concern working (sub)programs that can be tested by the students to observe their behavior, they can be well-documented and supplied with extra information, and questions about their workings as well as instructions to modify or complete them may be added. Second, the functions and workings of learned programming plans may be further clarified in the examples. In fact, the presented solutions may be annotated by explicitly referring to the programming plans they use. Then, the students are both presented with single programming plans during instruction and with compositions of - possibly nested - plans in real programs during practice. This is considered to be particularly important because the acquisition of programming plans is required to reach proficiency in both the design and coding of programs. In program design, high level plans may be used to separate input, process and output; then, the problem can be further decomposed into parts that can be solved with other plans. In coding program lines, low level plans may be used to combine elementary commands with their arguments using the correct syntax.

Finally, there is ample opportunity in the completion strategy to vary the tasks, problems and solutions that are presented to the students. First, all kinds of tasks, such as using the editor, applying syntactic rules, interpreting programs, testing and debugging programs, modifying and extending programs, and generating (sub)programs appear in the course. In addition, problems are presented in combination with their (partial) solutions so that students are confronted with a wide variety of both programming problems and solutions that have the form of well-designed, working programs.

Summarizing, there are three reasons why practice in the completion strategy is expected to be more effective than practice in generation strategies: (a) the students are provided with worked examples in a natural way, (b) they are confronted with compositions of (possibly nested) programming plans, and (c) they have the opportunity to perform a wide variety of tasks and study many problems as well as solutions. In the next section, we will turn to the empirical support that can be given to the completion strategy.

EMPIRICAL SUPPORT FOR THE COMPLETION STRATEGY

In our own research, several experiments have been conducted that, directly or indirectly, support the usefulness of the completion strategy. In this article, the results of three experiments are presented and discussed. The first experiment is concerned with the cognitive style reflection-impulsivity; the results support the view that the completion strategy may be useful to force impulsives into a more reflective strategy. The second experiment relates to group work in introductory programming; the results indicate that testing and debugging programs are student activities with significant positive effects on both learning outcomes and desirable verbal interactions. Obviously, the completion strategy is an excellent way to evoke these activities. The third experiment is directly concerned with a comparison of learning outcomes in courses designed according to the completion strategy or the generation strategy; the completion strategy was found to be clearly superior to the generation strategy. In the following sections, we will briefly review the experiments.

Experiment 1: Reflection-impulsivity

Research on cognitive styles and learning outcomes in programming instruction can yield a model for explaining and predicting the relations between those two variables. Such a model allows educators to design instructional strategies that ameliorate the negative effects of certain cognitive styles while capitalizing on the strength of others.

The cognitive style reflection-impulsivity (Kagan, Rosman, Day, Albert, & Phillips, 1964; Messer, 1976) can be easily related to behavior and learning outcomes in an introductory programming course, as novices frequently attempt to go from a detail of the problem specification to the programming code, without consideration of how to solve the problem as a whole, how to plan the solution, or how to design the code; that is, they exhibit impulsive behavior. The primary goal of this experiment (Van Merriënboer, 1988) was to explore the relation between reflection- impulsivity and learning outcomes, in order to develop prescriptions for optimal instructional strategies.

Method
21 High school students from grades 10-11 volunteered for participation in an introductory 10-lesson programming course. Each weekly one-hour lesson consisted of the presentation of a small number of new language features of the computer language COMAL-80 (Christensen, 1982) along with some syntactic details and worked examples, after which students were engaged in independently writing programs.

Prior to the course, students' reflection-impulsivity styles were determined from their scores on a computer-controlled version of the Matching Familiar Figures Test (Van Merriënboer & Jelsma, 1988). After the course, two learning outcomes were established for each student: (a) factual knowledge test score, to measure the knowledge of language features and syntax of COMAL-80, and (b) program comprehension test score, to measure the understanding of actions and structures in complete COMAL-80 programs. The factual knowledge test consisted of 24 multiple choice items concerning isolated program lines; the program comprehension test consisted of 18 multiple choice items concerning functionally related program lines in complete programs.

Results
No correlation between the cognitive style and the factual knowledge test scores could be observed, $r = -.05$; however, a significant correlation between reflection-impulsivity and the program comprehension test scores was found, $r = .39$, $p < .05$. For both tests, the percentages of correctly answered items for

reflective and impulsive subjects are presented in Figure 1. The effect due to cognitive style on the program comprehension test is significant according to a Mann-Whitney test, $U = 10$, $p < .05$. As may further be seen from the figure, the cognitive style has little effect on the acquired factual knowledge about the language.

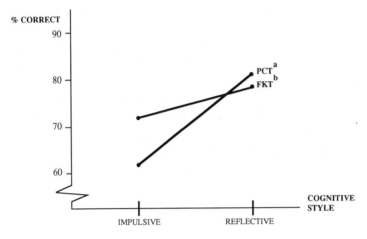

Figure 1. Percentages of correct items on the Factual Knowledge Test (FKT) and the Program Comprehension Test (PCT) for Impulsive and Reflective subjects.

From the literature, it is known that it is quite possible to force impulsives into a more reflective strategy through exposure to particular instructional materials (e.g., Clements, 1986). In the present course, students were free to choose their own problem solving strategy to a large extent. In contrast, the modification and amplification of programs in the completion strategy will require a thorough understanding of structures that combine several language features, that is, it will force the students into a more reflective strategy. Consequently, it is hypothesized on the basis of this study that the completion strategy will optimize problem solving approaches and result in better learning outcomes.

Experiment 2: Group Work

Both for practical reasons and because of the apparent effectiveness of cooperative learning, students who are engaged in introductory programming often work in small groups on a computer. The goal of this study (Krammer & Van Merriënboer, 1988) was to explore causal relationships between input variables (prior experience, group heterogeneity), student activities (analyzing the problem, testing and debugging the program), student-to-student interactions (tutoring, scientific debate) and learning outcomes (factual knowledge of the language, skill in program generation) in courses where students work in pairs on a computer.

Johnson & Johnson (1979) ascribe the effectiveness of cooperative learning to controversies between group members leading to scientific debate; such controversies can be expected in homogeneous groups. Other investigators (Peterson & Swing, 1985; Webb, 1982, 1984) study asking questions and explaining answers from which both tutors and students are supposed to gain in understanding; such tutoring may be expected in heterogeneous groups.

Method
48 high school students from grades 10-11 were divided into heterogeneous and homogeneous pairs according to their perceptions of own and peers' abilities; questionnaires were used to establish the perceptions. The programming course consisted of eight lessons using four textbooks (Van Merriënboer, 1986) that each covered two lessons on COMAL-80. Each pair was audio-recorded during the first five lessons. Two recorded lessons per pair were coded by two trained observers using the OCLI observation system (Observation of Cooperative Learning of Informatics; Krammer, 1987), which was implemented on a portable microcomputer. The observers had to code two facets every three seconds: Student activity (10 categories, including analyzing the problem and testing and debugging the program) and verbal interaction (16 categories, including tutoring and debate).

Both after four lessons and after eight lessons an 18-item multiple choice, factual knowledge test and a program-generation test were administered. The program-generation tests were scored according to a complex evaluation form in which number of correct and incorrect lines, the application of eight critical features, and the overall correctness were weighted.

Results
With student pairs as units of analysis, eight variables were put into a path analysis. The presumed model and the main results are depicted in Figure 2. The negative influence of heterogeneity on debate was expected, because in heterogeneous groups a controversy will be conceived by the students as a simple misconception of the less able student that can be cured by tutoring; in homogeneous groups a controversy will need a real debate.

The negative influence of both tutoring and debate on program generation is contrary to the generally accepted theory. In this study, no team-building activities took place before the actual instruction; as a possible explanation, this may have caused suboptimal interactive behavior of the pairs, and so the unexpected negative influence of the interaction variables on learning outcomes.

An important result is the central role of the student activity testing and debugging. Heterogeneity positively influences this variable, which can be interpreted by assuming that students preferably give explanations by using the program and showing how it works. Also, testing and debugging appears to cause tutoring and debate. This can be interpreted analogous to the former interpretation: While trying out a program, students may observe differences between their expectations and the actual behavior of the program, causing cognitive conflicts and leading to debates and tutoring situations. Finally, the positive influences of testing and debugging on learning outcomes may be explained by the good opportunities to cure misconceptions. As the completion strategy heavily emphasizes testing and debugging activities, it is expected to evoke desirable verbal interactions as well as to result in better learning outcomes.

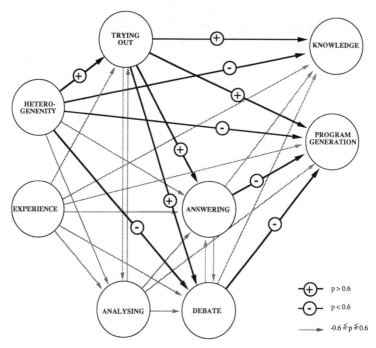

Figure 2. The strongest causal paths between Input, Activity, Interaction, and Outcome variables.

Experiment 3: Program Completion versus Program Generation

In this experiment (Van Merriënboer, in press), the expected advantage of the completion strategy on learning outcomes was directly studied by comparing it to a more traditional strategy that emphasized the design and coding of new programs.

Method

Two matched groups of 28 and 29 high school students from grades 10-11 participated in an introductory course that was designed according to either the completion strategy or the generation strategy. The goal of the course was the acquisition of some elementary program generation skills in five modules of two lessons each. For the generation strategy, each module consisted of three parts: (a) the presentation of some factual information about the programming language COMAL-80, (b) a model solution that demonstrated the generation of a program, and (c) a generation assignment that required the design and coding of a complete program. For the completion strategy, each module consisted of only two parts: (a) factual information, identical to that in the generation strategy, and (b) four completion assignments that consisted of a problem specification, a (partial) program that was available on disk, and some questions concerning the working of the program and instructions to modify or complete it.

After the course, a program construction test consisting of two programming problems was administered to measure skill in designing and coding new programs. Both programs that had to be constructed required, in addition to some specific characteristics, the use of 12 language features or programming concepts. For each program, the numbers of correctly and incorrectly coded lines were counted. In addition, two trained observers scored the correct use of each of the language features that had to be present in the programs as true or false, so that the overall quality of each program could be computed as the number of true categories. Finally, the observers scored the semantic correctness of each program on a 5-point scale.

Results
The medians for the percentages of incorrectly coded lines were 13.6% for the completion group and 24.1% for the generation group; according to a Wilcoxon signed rank test, this difference is significant, $W = 26$, $p < .05$. Figure 3 displays for both groups the percentages of programs in which the learned language features were used correctly. As may be seen from this figure, the completion group was superior to the generation group for all features, with exception of the use of conditionals. The medians for the overall quality of the programs were 15 for the completion group and 10 for the generation group, $W = 13$, $p < .01$. Concerning the semantic correctness of the programs, the subjects could reach a maximum score of 10 points if both constructed programs were semantically as well as syntactically correct; the completion group was superior to the generation group: The medians were, respectively, 6 and 5, $W = 26$, $p < .05$.

In short, the results on learning outcomes of this study clearly supported the view that the completion strategy is superior to a traditional strategy that emphasizes the complete generation of new programs. Further, the completion strategy was characterized by a lower mortality of subjects, in particular for female students with low prior knowledge of computers. And finally, the difficulty of the course as judged by the students remained constant for the completion strategy, but increased for the generation strategy. These results

assignments during the course; processing load is easier to control by varying the complexity of student activities, such as reading, tracing, modification, and completion.

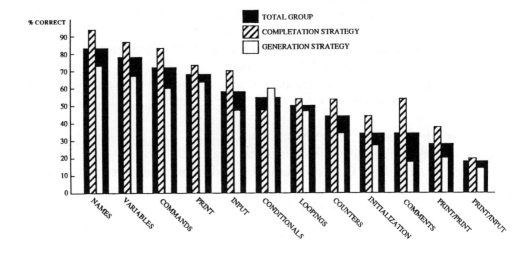

Figure 3. Percentages of programs for the Completion Strategy and the Generation Strategy in which programming concepts and language features are used correctly.

GENERAL DISCUSSION

The results of the reported studies consolidated our theoretical expectation that the completion strategy is effective for teaching introductory computer programming. Two experiments yielded indirect support. First, the completion strategy seems to be useful to force impulsives into a more reflective strategy; second, it evokes testing and debugging behavior, which has major positive influences on both desirable verbal interactions between students and learning outcomes. The third experiment yielded direct support to effectiveness of the completion strategy; with regard to learning outcomes, it was found to be clearly superior to a strategy that emphasized the generation of new, complete programs.

In relating the experimental data to the theory of programming plans, the first experiment supports the view that a reflective strategy positively affects the development of such plans. Impulsives seem to code a program line as soon as they associate a certain detail in the problem description with a newly learned language feature; after coding a program, their debugging is essentially a process of piecing the language features together in different ways. As a result, their understanding of programs remains basically at the level of a single line. On the contrary, reflectives consider different possible solutions to the problem before they code a number of functionally related levels of a single line. On the contrary, reflectives consider different possible solutions to the problem before they code a number of functionally related program lines; this advanced planning is helpful in developing programming plans that combine language features in larger patterns of code. Consequently, no difference in learning outcomes occurs as far as knowledge restricted to a single line level is concerned, but reflectives are superior to impulsives in program comprehension as this supposes the understanding of the working of blocks of functionally related program lines. As the completion strategy forces students to study partial programs before they start coding, it seems suitable to force them into a more reflective strategy.

The second experiment stressed the central role of student activities such as exploring programs, testing and debugging programs, and using programs to explain to pair mates how they work. These activities play a central role in the completion strategy and positively influence learning outcomes; furthermore, these activities seem to stimulate interactions between students that are expected to have a positive effect on learning outcomes too. As in the first experiment, the effects on learning outcomes can be well explained by the availability of correct programming plans. In our view, the good opportunities to cure misconceptions during testing and debugging are largely responsible for the development of such programming plans and the procedural skills to compose programs out of these plans.

As a result of the third experiment, there is more direct evidence that the completion strategy facilitated the development of programming plans. First, the percentage of correctly coded program lines was higher for the completion group. This may be well explained by the availability of templates that offer structures to code statements that combine basic commands with their arguments using the correct syntax. Second, looping structures in the completion group were more often combined with proper initializations above the loop as well as a correct use of counter variables and/or running totals within the loop; obviously, the completion strategy yields better developed templates to combine iterations with related concepts. Finally, the completion strategy leads to better developed general templates of what a well-coded program should look like. For example, comments to indicate the scope of the program and the goals of certain parts were more common in the completion group.

It is relatively easy to relate the results of the reported experiments to our theoretical framework. First, the presentation of partial, working (sub)programs seems to be worthwhile. It is shown that testing and debugging such programs is an important factor to reach proficiency in programming and that it is a strong method to force students to study well-designed solutions. Second, there is evidence that the constant confrontation with compositions of templates in real programs, and the possibilities to experiment with those programs and to discuss them with other students, leads to better developed programming plans and thus higher learning outcomes. Finally, the completion strategy offers much opportunities to vary the tasks that are assigned to the students; the students are confronted with many well-designed solutions, and it is yet possible to keep the difficulty of the course constant by assigning increasingly difficult tasks, such as tracing and predicting outcomes, making minor changes, completing programs, designing and coding subprograms, etc.

In future research, the results of the reported studies will have to be integrated in a comprehensive framework. A first question to be answered is whether the completion strategy actually interacts with the cognitive style reflection-impulsivity. Based on the aforementioned interpretation of results, it is expected that courses designed according to the completion strategy will show a significant increase in learning outcomes, especially for students with an impulsive style. Second, in addition to learning outcomes, the activities and verbal interactions of students who are working according to either the completion or the generation strategy will have to be compared. Thus, whereas there is some evidence for the superiority of the completion strategy over other strategies, further research is certainly needed to explain the responsible mechanisms.

Note

1.   The "completion strategy" may be seen as an instance of the "reading approach", as described in a previous article (Van Merriënboer & Krammer, 1987).

REFERENCES

Adelson, B. (1981). Problem solving and the development of abstract categories in programming languages. *Memory and Cognition*, *9*, 422-433.

Anderson, J.R., Boyle, C.F., Corbett, A., & Lewis, M. (1986). *Cognitive modelling and intelligent tutoring* (Tech. Rep. No. ONR-86-1). Pittsburgh, PA: Carnegie-Mellon University, Psychology Department.

Anderson, J.R, Farrell, R., & Sauers, R. (1984). Learning to program in LISP. *Cognitive Science*, *8*, 87-129.

Atwood, M.E., Turner, A.A., Ramsey, H.R., Hooper, J.N., & Sidorsky, R.C. (1979). *An explorative study of the cognitive structures underlying the comprehension of software design problems* (Tech. Rep. No. 392). Alexandria, VA: US Army Research Institute for the Behavioral and Social Sciences.

Barfield, W. (1986). Expert-novice differences for software: Implications for problem-solving and knowledge acquisition. *Behavior and Information*, *5*, 15-29.

Brooks, R. (1977). Towards a theory of the cognitive processes in computer programming. *International Journal of Man-Machine Studies*, *9*, 737-751.

Christensen, B.R. (1982). *Beginning Comal.* Chichester: Ellis Horwood.

Clements, D.H. (1986). Effects of Logo and CAI environments on cognition and creativity. *Journal of Educational Psychology, 78,* 309-318.

Dalbey, J., & Linn, M.C. (1985). The demands and requirements of computer programming: A literature review. *Journal of Educational Computing Research, 1,* 253-274.

Dalbey, J., Tourniaire, F., & Linn, M.C. (1985). *Making programming instruction cognitively demanding: An intervention study (ACCCEL Report).* Berkeley: University of California, Lawrence Hall of Science.

Deimel, L.E., & Moffat, D.V. (1982). A more analytical approach to teaching the introductory programming course. In J. Smith & M. Schuster (Eds.), *Proceedings of the NECC* (pp. 114-118). Columbia: The University of Missouri.

DuBoulay, B. (1986). Some difficulties of learning to program. *Journal of Educational Computing Research, 2,* 57-73.

DuBoulay, B., O'Shea, T., & Monk, J. (1981). The black box inside the glass box: Presenting computing concepts to novices. *International Journal of Man-Machine Studies, 14,* 237-249.

Ehrlich, K., & Soloway, E. (1984). An empirical investigation of the tacit plan knowledge in programming. In J. Thomas & M.L. Schneider (Eds.), *Human factors in computer systems* (pp. 113-133). Norwood, NJ: Ablex Publishing Corp.

Jeffries, R. Turner, A.A., Polson, P.G., & Atwood, M.E. (1981). The processes involved in designing software. In J.R. Anderson (Ed.), *Cognitive skills and their acquisition* (pp. 255-284). Hillsdale, NJ: Erlbaum Associates.

Johnson, D.W., & Johnson, R.T. (1979). Controversy and learning. *Review of Educational Research, 49,* 51-70.

Kagan, J., Rosman, B.L., Day, D., Albert, J., & Phillips, W. (1964). Information processing in the child: Significance of analytic and reflective attitudes. *Psychological Monographs, 78*(1, Whole No. 578).

Krammer, H.P.M. (1987). *Observatie van Coöperatief Leren bij Informatica: Het OCLI-instrument* (IST-MEMO-87-05) [Observation of Cooperative Learning of Informatics: The OCLI instrument]. Enschede, The Netherlands: University of Twente, Department of Education.

Krammer, H.P.M., & Van Merriënboer, J.J.G. (1988). *Causal relationships between group heterogeneity, activities, verbal interaction, and learning outcomes in an introductory programming course.* Paper presented at the Convention of the International Association for the Study of Cooperation in Education, Tel Aviv, July 5-8.

Kurland, D.M., Pea, R.D., Clement, C., & Mawby, R. (1986). A study of the development of programming ability and thinking skills in high school students. *Journal of Educational Computing Research, 2,* 429-485.

Linn, M.C. (1985). The cognitive consequences of programming instruction in classrooms. *Educational Researcher, 14*(5), 14-29.

Linn, M.C., Sloane, K.D., & Clancey, M.J. (1987). Ideal and actual outcomes from precollege Pascal instruction. *Journal of Research in Science Teaching, 24,* 467-490.

Mayer, R.E. (1975). Different problem-solving competencies established in learning computer programming with and without meaningful models. *Journal of Educational Psychology, 67,* 725-734.

Mayer, R.E. (1976). Some conditions of meaningful learning for computer programming: Advanced organizers and subject control of frame order. *Journal of Educational Psychology, 68,* 143-150.

Mayer, R.E., & Bromage, B. (1980). Different recall protocols for technical text due to advance organizers. *Journal of Educational Psychology, 72,* 209-225.

McKeithen, K.B., Reitman, J.S., Rueter, H.H., & Hirtle, S.C. (1981). Knowledge organization and skill differences in computer programmers. *Cognitive Psychology, 13,* 307-325.

Messer, S.B. (1976). Reflection-Impulsivity: A review. *Psychological Bulletin, 83,* 1026-1052.

Pea, R.D. (1986). Language-independent conceptual "bugs" in novice programming. *Journal of Educational Computing Research, 2,* 25-36.

Pea, R.D., & Kurland, D.M. (1984). On the cognitive effects of learning computer programming. *New Ideas in Psychology, 2,* 137-168.

Perkins, D.N., Hancock, C., Hobbs, R., Martin, F., & Simmons, R. (1986). Conditions of learning in novice programmers. *Journal of Educational Computing Research, 2,* 37-56.

Peterson, P.L., & Swing, S.R. (1985). Students' cognitions as mediators of the effectiveness of small-group learning. *Journal of Educational Psychology, 77,* 299-312.

Pintrich, P.R., Berger, C.F., & Stemmer, P.M. (1987). Students' programming behavior in a Pascal course. *Journal of Research in Science Teaching, 24,* 451-466.

Resnick, L.B., & Ford, W.W. (1981). *The psychology of mathematics for instruction.* Hillsdale, NJ: Erlbaum Associates.

Shneiderman, B. (1976). Exploratory experiments in programmer behavior. *International Journal of Computer and Information Sciences, 5,* 123-143.

Shneiderman, B. (1977). Measuring computer program quality and comprehension. *International Journal of Man-Machine Studies, 9,* 46-59.

Soloway, E. (1985). From problems to programs via plans: The content and structure of knowledge for introductory LISP programming. *Journal of Educational Computing Research, 1,* 157-172.

Van Merriënboer, J.J.G. (1986). *Programmeren in COMAL (Experimental textbook)* [Programming in COMAL]. Enschede, The Netherlands: University of Twente, Department of Education.

Van Merriënboer, J.J.G. (1988). Relationship between cognitive learning style and achievement in an introductory computer programming course. *Journal of Research on Computing in Education, 21,* 181-186.

Van Merriënboer, J.J.G. (in press). Strategies for programming instruction in high school: Program completion vs. program generation. *Journal of Educational Computing Research.*

Van Merriënboer, J.J.G., & Jelsma, O. (1988). The matching familiar figures test: Computer or experimenter controlled administration? *Educational and Psychological Measurement, 48,* 161-164.

Van Merriënboer, J.J.G., & Krammer, H.P.M. (1987). Instructional strategies and tactics for the design of introductory computer programming courses in high school. *Instructional Science, 16,* 251-285.

Webb, N.M. (1982). Student interaction and learning in small groups. *Review of Educational Research, 52,* 421-445.

Webb, N.M. (1984). Microcomputer learning in small groups: Cognitive requirements and group processes. *Journal of Educational Psychology, 76,* 1076-1088.

Weiser, M., & Shertz, J. (1983). Programming problem representation in novice and expert programmers. *International Journal of Man-Machine Studies, 19,* 391-398.

4

THE EFFECTS OF TEACHER TRAINING DESIGNED ON THE BASIS OF A TEACHING SCRIPT

Pieter C. van der Sijde
University of Twente

ABSTRACT

In this chapter the notion of a teaching script is introduced as a design theory for classroom teaching. Starting out from a teaching script a one-day training course for teachers is designed and executed. The effects of this training course are evaluated in two experiments. In the first experiment the effects of the training on the teaching behavior are evaluated, and in the second, the effects on the student's learning outcomes. It appeared that the training did bring about changes in teaching behavior, and, it had effect on the student's learning outcomes.

INTRODUCTION

Teaching is a complex cognitive skill. To be more precise, teaching is problem solving in a relatively ill-structured, dynamic environment. Classroom teaching consists of a number of linked problem situations: the solution of one problem situation directly influences the next problem situation.

Considering teaching as a cognitive skill makes it amenable to analysis in a manner similar to other cognitive skills. Every cognitive skill has at least two consecutive stages: planning and execution (Anderson, Greeno, Kline, & Neves, 1981). In the first stage a plan is made to solve the problem and in the second stage the plan is translated into actions to actually solve the problem.

If teaching is considered a cognitive skill, it follows that some teachers are more skilled than others. This led to a number of studies investigating teaching expertise (Berliner, 1986; Berliner & Carter, 1986; Leinhardt, 1986 a and b; Leinhardt & Greeno, 1986; Leinhardt & Smith, 1985), and these studies have been conducted in the same way as investigations into, for example, medical expertise (Johnson, Duran, Hassebrock, Moller, Prietula, Feltovich & Swanson, 1981; Epstein, Shulman & Sprafka, 1978). The renewed impetus for the study of expertise has been given by Glaser (1976). He mentions the analysis of competent performance as one of the components of a psychology of instruction: what has a competent performer in a subject-matter domain learned that distinguishes him from a novice? The analysis of competent performance gives rise to two lines of research: the study of the differences between novices and experts, and the analysis of the expert-performer.

The study of teaching competence poses a number of problems which have to be solved. Berliner (1986) mentions three major problems. The first problem concerns criteria for identification of experts: it is rather easy to identify a chess grand master (he won thousands of games in national and international contests), a top athlete (someone who holds a world record), a top scientist (a Nobel Prize winner) and even a highly talented concert pianist can be identified, but what about the expert teacher? Are there any objective criteria to identify the expert teacher? The second problem is the confounding of experience and expertise. Who is the expert? Is the expert the one with experience? Yes, of course, but the statement should be irreversible. It should not be the case, that the one with a lot of experience automatically is the expert. The final problem concerns the knowledge systems used in teaching. What is the specific knowledge of a teacher? It is obvious that the knowledge of a chess grand master lies in chess, and to study expertise in physics one studies the way an expert solves physics problems. How to study expertise in classroom teaching if one hardly knows what knowledge systems are involved? Of course subject matter knowledge is involved, and, as Berliner (1986) states, knowledge of organization, and classroom management. Leinhardt and Greeno (1986) also distinguish two knowledge systems: lesson structure knowledge and subject matter knowledge.Leinhardt and Smith (1985) assume that expertise involved in the cognitive aspects of teaching has two core areas of knowledge: lesson structure knowledge and subject matter knowledge. The first is the knowledge required to construct and conduct a lesson, and the second is the knowledge of the content to be taught.

We assume that the knowledge systems involved in teaching are *lesson organization knowledge* (the skills to plan a lesson), subject matter knowledge (the knowledge of the content), *instruction knowledge* (the skill to explain the material clearly, to pose questions, to give feedback), and *classroom management knowledge* (the skills to run a lesson smoothly).

The main feature of the skilled teachers' knowledge structure is a set of schemata for teaching activities. Instead of regarding teaching as based on a set of schemata, it can also be regarded as based on a particular set of schemata, namely a script, which is an operational plan.

If teaching can be characterized as scripted behavior then a teacher should have a (more or less) stable cognitive representation of what teaching is (his own particular teaching script), which guides his interactive teaching

(Shavelson & Stern, 1981), *after* he entered the script. Such teaching scripts are routinized. Once begun, they typically are carried out. This script is taught to the teacher in his teacher training course(s), containing some or all of the elements (or scenes) of the script, and routinized through experience. Having a stable cognitive representation does not mean that one has the correct and complete or the ideal script. For example a teaching script for teaching mathematics could have five different scenes:(1) Homework check; (2) Presentation; (3) Monitored practice; (4) Guided practice; (5) Tutoring. Each scene has its own activities which are specific to that particular scene. An ideal lesson, in that context, must contain each of the five scenes. Each scene addresses a unique aspect of the learning-teaching process. Because there are differences between teachers (Good, Biddle & Brophy, 1975), there are variants of the script which arise from different sequences. For example, some teachers like to start a lesson with an explanation of new concepts and then proceed with the correction of homework so the students who did not encounter problems can already start on their new homework assignments. This means that in the script the first two scenes are reversed. Another example is that the scenes on seatwork are sometimes considered the same, although there are some major differences.

The way a script is executed reflects the way the script is represented in memory. There are two conceptions of how scripts are represented. The first regards a script as a sequential representation of the scenes (Figure 1), and the second (Figure 2) expresses the importance of the scenes in the script. The latter is a centrality representation (Galambos & Rips, 1982). For the teaching script we adopt the second conception, the centrality representation of scenes in the teaching script, because it has the flexibility to deal with individual differences among teachers.

Because of the differences among teachers and in subject matter, which affect the representation of teaching scripts, there will be differences in executing the script. These differences become observable in differences in the orderings of the scenes during the execution, and also in the absence of scenes.

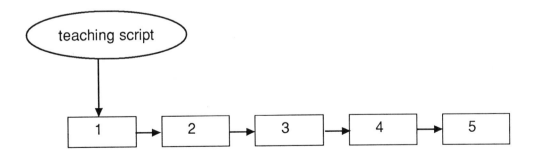

Figure 1. A sequential representation of a script.

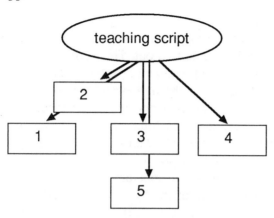

Figure 2. A centrality representation of a script.

THE TEACHER TRAINING

On basis of the teaching script outlined above a one-day teacher training program for mathematics teachers is designed. In teaching, four knowledge systems are involved, of which lesson organization knowledge is reflected in the teaching script. By restricting ourselves to mathematics teachers there is no need to include subject matter knowledge in the teacher training program. This means that classroom management knowledge and instruction knowledge should also be part of the program.

Classroom management knowledge is script-specific (classroom management techniques are used in order to carry out the script), while instruction is scene-specific (each scene requires different instruction).

The theoretical foundation for classroom management was found in the works of Kounin (1970). He concluded from his studies into classroom management behavior that there are six important management strategies: withitness ("eyes in the back"), overlapping ("doing two thing at the same time"), smoothness and jerkiness (with reference to the course of the lesson), momentum and slowdown ("keep a continuous pace"), group focus ("keep the attention to the group"), and anti-satiation ("take care that the students do not get satiated"). Kounin's theory is cognitively interpretated in Van der Sijde (1985a, 1987), and on the basis of this interpretation recommendations or rules are formulated which are included in the program. Further from Arlin (1979) it appeared that the transitions (from scene to scene) should be as smooth as possible in order to minimize off-task behavior. These rules are summarized in Table 1; an elaboration on these rules can be found in Van der Sijde (1985b).

The recommendations on instruction are scene-specific. These recommendations or rules are based on three sources. The first source is the Dutch Classroom Environment Study carried out by Krammer and Tomic of our University (Krammer, 1984; Tomic, 1985) in which the correlations between teacher behavior and students' learning outcomes were investigated. The second source is the results of research carried out in the same research tradition as the Classroom Environment Study (for a compilation, see Gage, 1985). The third source contains, in our terminology, scene-specific research (such as research on homework, presentation, etc.). These three sources led to the formulation of scene-specific rules (see Table 2). An elaboration of these rules can be found in Van der Sijde (1985).

Table 1
Rules on classroom management based on Kounin (1970)

Use a beginning-of-the-lesson signal;
Make transitions between lesson scenes as smooth as possible;
Make sure there is a continuous stream of activities in the classroom;
Be withit;
Maintain group focus;
Let students be responsible for their work.

Table 2
Scene-specific instructional recommendations

Review of homework	. deal with all homework assignments . check all homework assignments
Presentation	. give a review of relevant concepts . refresh prior knowledge . use examples . indicate what is important and what is not
Monitored practice	. give a short, clear assignment directed to knowledge, understanding or application . check the assignment . react positively to the students
Guided practice	. give probes . redirect questions
Homework/Tutoring	. give enough time at the end of a lesson to allow the students to start their homework . give attention to students who need extra attention

THE IMPLEMENTATION STUDY

The purpose of this study is tracing the effect of changes in the teaching script (as a result of training) on the actual teaching behavior. As Duffy and Roehler (1985) state, it is difficult to change teachers and the teachers particularly resist complex, conceptual longitudinal changes; they don't resist changes in management routines and temporary changes. The observations of Duffy and Roehler (1985) contrast with the results of a study by Gliesman (1985). He found that teachers could make changes in their complex teaching behavior through conceptual methods of training. A conceptual method of training is based upon full understanding of a teaching skill, so it directly facilitates use of the skill. It appears from the two studies mentioned that (disregarding the nature of the change) it is possible to change teacher behavior.

It is necessary to study the implementation of the training for several reasons, of which the most important one, as formulated by Fullan and Pomfret (1977), is, that unless the implementation is studied separately, it may be difficult to interpret learning outcomes and to relate these to possible determinants.

Method

Subjects
Ten mathematics teachers using the textbook *Sigma* in the 8th grade (2nd grade Havo/Vwo) voluntarily participated in this experiment (NB: about 20 teachers were approached and asked to participate). During the experiment one teacher got ill for an extended period of time; the data of this teacher were excluded from the analysis. All teachers were male, their mean number of years of experience as a teacher was 11.3 years (standard deviation: 6.2), and they worked at schools in the vicinity of the University of Twente.

Procedure
In the period March-April 1986 observation data of six teachers were sampled (using the observation instrument TOOL-W, see Van der Sijde, 1985c) by six trained observers during six lessons (two lessons per week) and, due to circumstances, the data of the three other teachers were collected during three lessons (these teachers started their participation after the experiment had already begun). The teachers then visited our institute in their Easter-holiday period for the one-day-inservice training. In the period following the Easter-holidays (April-May 1986) they were again observed for 6 lessons (one lesson per week). To inform the teachers about their teaching behavior in the period April-May (after the training), they received, within 24 hours, a letter with feedback on their lesson regarding the presence of scenes, classroom management, and instruction. After the experiment had been completed the teachers again visited the institute for an informal gathering to evaluate the

experiment. A number of lessons (n=17) was observed by two observers in order to calculate interobserver agreement.

Design and data
The design used in this study is a one group pretest-posttest design. Although such a design has a number of disadvantages (see Campbell & Stanley, 1966) we decided to use this particular design, because before and after the training more than one observation is used to calculate the mean score.

In order to study how the teaching script was executed the variable L is constructed. The L-score is defined as 5 minus the number of observed scenes in a lesson; in the ideal lesson L= 0.

Further, in TOOL-W a number of Kouninian variables are operationalized. Only the Kouninian variables have been reported in the results. Withitness is operationalized in low inference (directly observable) variables. These low inference variables are: the teacher watches the student (direction of gaze is toward the pupils), the teacher changes place (he takes another position in the classroom), the teacher looks at a particular student to indicate he has seen that the pupil shows inappropriate behavior, the teacher rebukes a student and the teacher suggests alternative behavior to a student who shows inappropriate behavior. The number of times the teacher performs such behavior is observed before and after the training. Withitness is the standardized sum of the five low inference behaviors mentioned. Group alerting is operationalized by the number of times the teacher alerts the class, e.g. with "this is important" or "pay attention". Learner accountability is operationalized by the number of times a teacher asks for progress made by the pupils (e.g. "who has completed ....", "who is not ready by now?").

The increase (or decrease) on the management and instruction behavior is expressed as the effect size. Effect size E is defined as $(X_A - X_B/sd_B)$, where X_A is the mean score after the training, X_B is the mean score before the training and sd_B is the standard deviation of X_B (Walberg,1984).

Results

Interobserver agreement
During the observation periods of the experiment mean interobserver agreement was calculated using Cohen's kappa (Cohen, 1962). The kappa (κ) for the direction of gaze is: κ= 0.50; for the lesson phases: κ= 0.92; for the classroom management behavior: κ= 0.73; and for the instruction behavior: κ= 0.52.

Execution of the script
In the training the script approach of teaching was discussed and the teachers were asked to implement its consequence model. Based on the observed lessons the implementation score (L) of the script was calculated and the

scores before and after the training were compared. The mean L-score before the training is 2.3, while after the training the L-score is 1.6. After the training there is a significant change towards more lessons with more scenes present than before the training, $\chi^2(8) = 34.88$ (p < .01). Table 3 presents the average amount of time the teachers spent on each lesson phase before and after the training.

Table 3
Time engaged in minutes before and after the training in each of the scenes of the script

scene	before	after	p*
review of homework	22.4	16.6	<.10
presentation	5.4	8.4	<.05
monitored practice	3.4	7.2	<.05
guided practice	2.2	4.4	<.05
homework/tutoring	4.8	.6.4	>.10

*t-test, one-tailed.

There is an increase in time spent on instruction from approximately 38.2 minutes to approximately 43 minutes. Further, there is a significant decrease in time spent on the "review of homework", and a significant increase in time spent on "presentation", "monitored practice" and "guided practice".

The implementation of classroom management behavior
The mean withitness-score and its standard deviation before the training are 0.02 and 2.41, and, after the training 0.16 and 2.4 respectively. The effect size E of the training on withitness is E = 0.06. The mean group-alerting score and its standard deviation before the training are -0.02 and 1.4, and, afterwards -0.06 and 1.2 respectively, the effect size of group-alerting is E = -0.01. Before the training the mean score for learner accountability and its standard deviation are -0.001 and 1.0, and, afterwards -0.02 and 1.0 respectively. The effect is E = -0.02.

Looking at the individual teachers, withitness-behavior improved significantly (with more then one standard deviation) for 5 out of 9 teachers, the same was observed for group-alerting and learner accountability behaviors.

Implementation of the instruction behavior
Instruction is divided into three components: explanation, questions, and feedback. According to our recommendations, every lesson, as far as it concerns the phase "presentation", should contain a review of relevant concepts. Before the training, this was done in each lesson by 4 teachers; after

the training by 7 teachers. Instead of the teacher performing a review, students can also be asked to do this. Before the training, the mean time per lesson during which the teacher was engaged in review questions like these was 2.4 sec., and after the training 2.8 sec. The effect size is $E = 0.28$. Another aspect of explaining is the use of the textbook. The mean amount of time per lesson the teacher referred to the textbook was 0.7 sec. before and after the training. Instead of referring to the textbook the teacher can also indicate (e.g. on the blackboard) what the important issues are. The training did not change teacher behavior on this aspect. Before the training hardly any time was spent on the use of examples (2.5 sec. per lesson); afterwards this was 0.85 sec/lesson. The effect is $E = 1.75$, and the difference is significant ($t_{16} = 2.00$, $p < .05$). Presentation should also contain a summary; two teachers did this during every lesson before the training, and after the training this was done by four teachers.

Questions form a second component of explanation. After the training the teachers used more higher level questions ($E = 1.13$; $t_{16} = 2.10$, $p < .05$) and now a difference was found with respect to recall or recognize questions ($E = -0.18$; $t_{16} = -0.44$, $p > .10$). Further, more, but not significantly more questions were redirected ($E = 0.56$; $t_{16} = 0.16$, $p > .10$). Moreover, there was a nonsignificant decrease on giving more than one probe ($E = 0.42$; $t_{16} = -1.11$, $p > .10$), and a nonsignificant increase of higher level questions during "presentation" was observed ($E = 0.48$; $t_{16} = 0.89$, $p > .10$). The most appropriate place for higher level questions is the "guided practice", during this scene an increase in such questions was observed ($E = 1.76$; $t_{16} = 1.95$, $p < .05$).

The third component of explanation is feedback. The effect size of positive feedback is $E = 0.17$ and of negative feedback, $E = 0.31$.

Discussion

The data on the use of time spent on a scene show that the training has caused a change. After the training more scenes were included in teaching. Monitored practice took about 3 minutes before the training and about 7.2 minutes after the training. There is an overall increase of effective time on task of approximately 5 minutes from 38 minutes to 43 minutes. One lesson lasts maximally 50 minutes and part of it is the change of classroom for the next lesson. This means that on the whole there is a substantial increase.

Important in this context is the adoption of the teaching script and its scenes by the teachers. The teaching script as presented in the training could be implemented by the participating teachers. This means that their teaching script did actually change. It can be concluded from Table 3 that the scenes "review of homework" and "presentation", together take 73% of the time spent on instructional activities. After the training these two scenes take about 58%.

This means that an average lesson contains more scenes, which is a result of the changes in the teaching scripts of the individual teachers.

Although the teachers participating in our experiment were very experienced (mean 11.3 years), they apparently were able and willing to implement the proposed behavior on classroom management (withitness, learner accountability, and group alerting)

The use of examples has a substantial effect size. Walberg (1984), in his meta-analysis of research, mentions "reinforcement" as having the greatest effect size, which is 1.17. Teachers did not conduct more reviews after the training than before.

On the whole, the teachers posed fewer lower-order questions and more higher level questions than before the training. An explanation for these findings is that the most appropriate place for posing recall or recognize questions is during presentation, but they are hard to formulate. It is easier (at least in mathematics) to formulate a question as a higher level questions, so an increase of higher- order questions (which probably were intended as lower-order questions) was observed.

Finally, we observed a nonsignificant increase in positive feedback, both in "feedback-good" and "feedback-good and the teacher repeats answer", and a decrease in negative feedback both in "feedback-wrong", "feedback-wrong and teacher answers the question himself".

As a general trend in inservice training, Fullan (1986) mentions that "one-shot workshops are widespread and ineffective". The training (plus the manual) was a "one-shot workshop" and, judging from the results, effective. The training in this study proposed changes in the teaching script and in the activities in each of its scenes. For each recommendation based on this script an explanation and evidence from research on teaching were given. In other words, the training was based on conceptual understanding of the content and its intention. Of course, the stress on conceptual understanding is one of the reasons why the training has been implemented. There is, however, another important reason, which is related to the nature of the recommendations. All recommendations are practical and most of them are derived from actual teaching behavior. Teachers combine information they receive (from researchers and educators) with what they already know, they restructure it and make it fit their perception of teaching reality (Duffy and Roehler, 1985). During the training session it appeared that the teachers already practiced some of the recommendations, not systematically, but in a rather random way. Thus, it already fit their knowledge structure. There was hardly any need to restructure the information.

The conclusion of this experiment is that the training developed on the basis of the teaching script, which is supported by empirical evidence, did change the actual teaching behavior, although not all dimensions of the teaching behavior did change. The fact that the teachers participating in this study were no novice teachers (far from it, in fact) makes it even more interesting. It means that when an innovation is adopted voluntarily, the implementation is more likely to occur, even in the case of experienced teachers who have probably routinized much of their teaching behavior. The results of this study do not give rise to changes in the manual prepared for the teacher training, although two aspects of the training content have to be dealt with more explicitly during the one-day teacher training. The first is the difference between lower and higher level questions, and the second is the difference between guided and monitored practice. Notwithstanding these facts, the results of this study indicate that in the next study, in which the effect of the training (of the teachers) on student achievement and attitude will be investigated, an effect on these can be ascribed to this training.

THE EFFECT OF THE TRAINING ON STUDENTS' LEARNING OUTCOMES

As described above, the training based on the teaching script did actually influence the behavior of the teachers in the classroom. But what about the effects on the students? It appeared from research (summarized by Gage, 1985) that trainings like ours also affects the learning outcomes (achievement and attitudes) of students. In this second experiment we set out to explore the effects of the training on the students.

Method

Subjects
About sixty teachers were approached to participate in this study, and thirty-three teachers volunteered to do so. All teachers taught mathematics in the 8th grade using the textbook *Sigma*. The subjects were assigned to four conditions. To condition one: n = 13 teachers, condition two: n = 8 teachers, condition three: n = 6 teachers, and condition four: n = 6 teachers one of whom dropped out. The teachers in conditions one and two participated in the experiment during the period September through March, while the teachers in conditions three and four only participated during the period December through March. The teachers were recruited in the vicinity of the University of Groningen, in the vicinity of the University of Delft, and in the vicinity of the University of Eindhoven.

Procedure
There are four experimental conditions. The teachers (and their classes) in condition one participated in a one-day-training course at the University. Shortly after the training a student achievement test and the student attitude test (containing scales to measure students' self-image and students' enjoyment of mathemathics) were administered in their classrooms. Then a number of lessons were observed during the period September - December,

and after the observations the same attitude test and a second achievement test were administered. After another period of 2 months (April) the same attitude test and a third achievement test were administered. Condition two resembles condition one except for the fact that the teachers did not receive the training before the observation period, but after the observations of the lessons (in January). The teachers in condition three and condition four participated during the period December-April. In December a student achievement test and the student attitude test were administered in their classrooms. Only the teachers in condition three received a copy of the training manual by mail. In April a student achievement test and the student attitude test were also administered in the classrooms of the teachers in conditions three and four. Conditions one and two are the experimental conditions, while Conditions three and four are the control conditions.

Results

Table 4 and Table 5 depict the results of the tests which were administered. The scores on the achievement tests administered in September show no significant difference between the conditions (Mann Whitney U: MWU=47), nor for the tests in December (MWU=42) and for the tests in April (MWU=44). The same holds for the attitude tests (enjoying mathematics: September: MWU=50, December: MWU=40, and April: MWU=41; self-image: September: MWU=50, December: MWU=44, and April: MWU=40.5). From the results, it appears that the training has an effect on students' learning outcomes. This effect becomes visible in the results of the standardized increase in scoring of the September achievement test to the April achievement test in favor of Condition 2 (Mann Whitney $U = 27$, $p < .10$). (NB: this increase does not become visible on the raw scores presented in Table 5, which shows the opposite: a decrease. Using the group mean and standard deviation the standardized scores were calculated). A second effect becomes visible when comparing the experimental conditions (Conditions 1 and 2) and the control conditions (Conditions 3 and 4) for the increase in scores from the December test to the April test with respect to students' self-image ($F_{(1,30)} = 4.83$; $p < .05$). No effects were found of mailing the manual to the teachers in Condition 3.

Discussion

The results show that the classroom means of the teachers in Conditions one and two are comparable for the attitude as well as the achievement scores, they do not differ significantly. This holds for the September tests as well as for the December and April tests. This is also the case for Conditions one, two, three and four on the December and April tests.

Table 4
Mean classroom scores and their standard deviations on the achievement tests

	September	December	April
Condition 1	.622 (.07)	.524 (.16)	.466 (.08)
Condition 2	.609 (.08)	.595 (.19)	.519 (.16)
Condition 3	--------	.493 (.17)	.420 (.11)
Condition 4	--------	.549 (.17)	.481 (.12)

Table 5
Mean classroom scores and their standard deviations on attitude (enjoying mathematics and self-image)

	September	December	April
Enjoying mathematics			
Condition 1	21.36 (1.79)	21.05 (2.00)	20.93 (1.76)
Condition 2	21.43 (1.32)	21.60 (1.13)	21.67 (1.19)
Condition 3	-----------	21.21 (1.75)	20.20 (1.75)
Condition 4	-----------	21.36 (1.64)	21.12 (1.61)
Self-image			
Condition 1	17.93 (1.66)	18.05 (1.74)	18.85 (2.42)
Condition 2	18.04 (0.90)	18.34 (0.84)	19.04 (1.51)
Condition 3	-----------	18.21 (1.74)	17.78 (2.10)
Condition 4	-----------	18.26 (1.45)	18.69 (1.96)

The increase in scores from the September tests to the December and April tests were studied to assess the effectiveness of the training. Comparing the difference in increase in mean classroom scores on the achievement test and the attitude tests between the teachers in the first experimental condition and the teachers in the second experimental condition, there is no significant difference in the period September- December. This is a remarkable result, because such a result has not been reported so far in other training studies. In the first part of our experiment we used a research design similar to those used in other studies (a nonequivalent control group design) and we did not find a positive effect of the training on the achievement and attitude scores in that first period.

The teachers in the first experimental condition behaved according to the teaching script, which took a central place in the training. This statement is supported by the results of the first experiment and it also appeared from the results presented in Van der Sijde (1987). This means that the changes in their actual teaching behavior did not have an effect on increase in scores on the test in the period September-December. Probably a period of approximately 2.5 months is too short. The teachers in the first experimental condition had to find out for themselves to what degree they already behaved according to the new teaching script. The difference in the increase in scores on the achievement test in the September-April period is significant and in favor of the second experimental condition. No effect was found on the increase in scores on the attitude tests. This means that the most effective condition is the one with the training after the observation period. There is an explanation for this effect. The teachers in the first condition participated in the training. Many of the recommendations and rules are plausible and in a sense familiar to the teacher, because some of them express what a good teacher *should* do. The teachers in the first condition were allowed to mix up what they *do* in the classroom and what they *should do* in the classroom. In other words, these teachers did not know to what extent their own teaching script resembled the teaching script proposed in the training. Because of this possible confusion, no indications for changes could be given (no data of classroom observation were available). The teachers in the second condition, however, were not allowed to confuse their actual teaching behavior with a desired teacher behavior. During the training all observation data were available and used. The teachers were confronted with the results of the classroom observations. In other words, these teachers received information (feedback) on how their teaching script resembled the teaching script proposed in the training, and as a result, concrete indications for change could be given. Probably the most effective design is the design in which training is given on two occasions: a first training before a period of observations, and a second training after a number of observations of lessons in which the same training, but tailored, is given to the teachers after two or three months.

If the teachers in the third and fourth conditions are compared on the increase in scores on the tests in the December-April period, there are no significant differences. This means that sending the training manual by mail did not affect the teaching behavior. The same results were obtained by Coladarci and Gage (1984).

This study, in conclusion, establishes that even a short teacher training course can successfully change the teachers' teaching script and subsequently their teaching behavior, which influences student achievement.

REFERENCES

Anderson, J.R., Greeno, J.G., Kline, P.J., & Neves, D.M. (1981). Acquisition of problem-solving skill. In Anderson, J.R. (Ed.), *Cognitive skills and their acquisition* (pp. 191-230). Hillsdale, NJ: Lawrence Erlbaum Associates.

Arlin, M. (1979). Teacher transition can disrupt timeflow in classrooms. *American Educational Research Journal, 16,* 42-56.

Berliner, D.C. (1986). In persuit of the expert pedagogue. *Educational Researcher, 15*(7), 5-13.

Berliner, D.C., & Carter, K.J. (1986). *Differences in processing classroom information by experts and novices*. Paper presented at the Conference of the International Study Association on Teacher Thinking, Leuven.

Campbell, D.T., & Stanley, J.C. (1966). *Experimental and quasi-experimental designs for research*. Chicago: Rand McNally.

Cohen, J. (1960). A coefficient of agreement for nominal scales. *Educational and Psychological Measurement, 20*, 37-46.

Coladarci, T., & Gage, N.L. (1984). Effects on a minimal intervention on teacher behavior and student achievement. *American Educational Research Journal, 21*, 539-555.

Duffy, G.G., & Roehler, L.R. (1985). *Constraints on teacher change*. East Lansing: Michigan State University. Institute for Research in Teaching.

Epstein, A.S., Shulman, L.S., & Sprafka, S.A. (1978). *Medical problem solving*. Cambridge: Harvard University Press.

Fullan, M., & Pomfret, A. (1977). Research on curriculum and instruction implementation. *Review of Educational Research, 47*, 335-397.

Gage, N.L. (1985). *Hard gains in the soft sciences*. Bloomington: Phi Delta Kappan.

Galambos, J.A., & Rips, L.J. (1982). Memory for routines. *Journal of Verbal Learning and Verbal Behavior, 21*, 260-281.

Glaser, R. (1976). Components of a psychology of instruction: Towards a science of design. *Review of Educational Research, 46*, 1-24.

Gliesman, D.H. (1985). *A study of change in complex teaching skills*. Paper presented at the Annual Meeting of the AERA, Chicago.

Good, T.L., Biddle, B.J., & Brophy, J.E. (1975). *Teachers make a difference*. New York: Holt, Rinehart & Winston.

Johnson, P.E., Duran, A.S., Hassebrock, F., Moller, J. Prietula, M., Feltovich, P.J., & Swanson, D.B. (1982). Expertise and error. *Cognitive Science, 6*, 235-283.

Kounin, J.S. (1979). *Discipline and group management*. New York: Holt, Rinehart & Winston.

Krammer, H.P.M. (1984). *Leerboek en leraar*. Harlingen: Flevodruk.

Leinhardt, G. (1986a). Expertise in mathematics teaching. *Educational Leadership, 43*, 28-33 (April).

Leinhardt, G. (1986b). Math lessons: a contrast of novice and expert competence. In J. Lowyck (Ed.), *Proceedings of the third congress of the International Study Association on Teacher Thinking*. Leuven: University of Leuven.

Leinhardt, G., & Greeno, J.G. (1986). The cognitive skill of teaching. *Journal of Educational Psychology, 78*, 75-95.

Leinhardt, G., & Smith, D. (1985). Expertise in mathematics instruction: subject matter knowledge. *Journal of Educational Psychology, 77*, 247-271.

Schank, R., & Abelson, R. (1977). *Scripts, plans, goals and understanding.* Hillsdale, NJ: Lawrence Erlbaum Associates.

Shavelson, R.J., & Stern, P. (1981). Research on teacher's pedagogical thoughts, judgements, decisions and behavior. *Review of Educational Research, 51,* 455-498.

Tomic, W. (1985). *Docentgedrag en leerresultaten.* Enschede: Universiteit Twente, Faculteit Toegepaste Onderwijskunde.

Van der Sijde, P.C. (1985a). *Classroom management als cognitief proces.* Paper gepresenteerd tijdens de ORD te Enschede.

Van der Sijde, P.C. (1985b). *Management en instructie in wiskundelessen.* Enschede: Universiteit Twente, Faculteit Toegepaste Onderwijskunde.

Van der Sijde, P.C. (1985c). *Het observatiesysteem TOOL-W.* Enschede: Universiteit Twente, Faculteit Toegepaste Onderwijskunde.

Van der Sijde, P.C. (1987). *Training the teaching script.* Almere: Versluys.

Walberg, H.J. (1984). Improving the productivity of American schools. *Educational Leadership, 41,* 19-27.

5

THE USE OF COLOUR TO STRUCTURE INSTRUCTIONAL TEXTS

Bernadette H.A.M. van Hout Wolters
Willeke M.J. Kerstjens
Pløn W. Verhagen
University of Twente

ABSTRACT

The design of printed instructional texts has been a subject of research for some considerable time. However, research on the use of colour in instructional texts is scarce. Yet text books are often printed in colour, although it increases the cost of production substantially.

In this study, it was investigated whether the systematic use of colour to distinguish thematic parts of an instructional text clarifies the structure of the content in such a way that it causes extra recall of the presented information as compared to the same text without colour. Also, the influence of verbal ability and cognitive style on recall was investigated. Further, students' valuation of the use of colour was determined. Subjects were 93 freshmen at a nurses' training college.

INTRODUCTION

For some considerable time now, the structuring of subject matter in printed instructional texts has been a subject of theoretical interest and research (see for instance Kulhavy, Schmid & Walker, 1977; Reigeluth & Stein, 1983). This research concerns the structuring of the content itself, as well as methods to clarify the content structure or to make it explicit by means of a certain text design (Jonassen, 1982, 1985). For this latter purpose, several techniques are available: the use of typography (bold type, italics, etc.), layout (line width, use of columns, extra line spacing, etc.), marking, colouring and numbering of parts of text. Although most of these instructional design techniques have been the subject of a substantial amount of research (Van Hout Wolters, 1986), much less attention is paid to the use of colour in instructional texts. A systematic survey of the literature carried out during the preparation of the present study (Kerstjens, 1988) confirmed this.

Colour is regularly used in text books, not only in illustrations, but also in the text itself. Publishers and authors obviously consider it useful to colour characters or their background in certain parts of the text, even if this increases production cost. Little is known about the instructional effect of colour. For the design of printed instructional materials, however, more knowledge about the effects of colour would be welcome.

Research on the use of colour in verbal contexts other than instructional texts is more readily available. Lamberski (1980) presents an overview of colour research between 1945 and 1980, in which attention is paid to "nonsense and meaningful word tasks" (for instance, tasks involving paired associates) and "prose tasks". In the latter type of task, colour is mainly used to give directions to young students who are learning how to read and spell. It appears that in general students prefer colour coding over other coding systems. Moreover, study results often appear to improve with the use of colour coding.

In a literature survey by Vroemen (1986), research is reviewed with respect to the design of colour screen computer displays. He distinguishes, as do other authors (for instance Hartley, 1978), a number of functions of colour:
- Coding; by colouring, meaning is added (as by colouring electrical wires).
- Structuring; colour clarifies the structure of data.
- Emphasizing; important aspects are emphasized by colouring.
- Cosmetics, aesthetics; colour is used to make the presentation more appealing.

The study by Vroemen (1986) showed that operators prefer a colour display over a monochrome display. It appears that by using colour, the speed and accuracy of their work can be improved, especially when complex displays and displays with high information density are involved. But the use of colour does not always have positive effects. After some training, colour displays appear not to yield better results than monochrome ones.

In addition to the literature studies mentioned, much literature is available from which general suggestions and design rules may be distilled with respect to the use of colour to present information. These relate to the number of colours to be used, the distinguishability of colours, specific colour choices, consistency of colour use and the use of background or character colours (e.g. Carter & Cahill, 1976; De Weert, 1985; Reising & Emerson, 1985). These suggestions and rules can be of relevance to the use of colour in instructional texts.

The research in this study concerns the use of colour as a design variable in structuring instructional texts. Colour is used to clarify the structure of the subject matter. Parts of the text which refer to specific themes are coloured with the same colour. It was expected that studying a coloured text would be positively evaluated (Lamberski, 1980; Vroemen, 1986).

It was also expected that structuring by colouring would positively influence the recall of specific facts and concepts from the text. The addition of colour would quickly make clear to the students how the text was structured. This structure might act as a "peg" ("retrieval schema", "subsumer") to store and retrieve the hierarchically lower ordered facts and concepts (see Shimmerlik, 1978). If the structure were less clear to the student, the "peg"-function would also be less clear. The influence of the use of colour in this way would be similar to the influence of the use of headings in texts (Lucas & Di Vesta, 1980). Merrill (1983) has called this phenomenon "isolation".

METHOD

Research questions

(1) Does the systematic colouring of thematically different parts of an instructional text lead to clarification of the structure of the content of the text in such a way that extra recall effects occur in comparison with the same text without colour?
(2) Does colouring of thematically different parts of an instructional text influence the valuation of studying the text by the students?

Subjects

Subjects were 93 freshmen of a nurses' training college. They were randomly assigned to the colour condition and the black-and-white condition, i.e. a "randomized group design" was used.

By means of a questionnaire, information was gathered about the students' previous schooling, their study results during their first year (the experiment was carried out near the end of the school year), and their sex. This information was used as general background information about the students and to check whether the randomly composed groups were equivalent with respect to these variables.

Materials

The instructional text used was entitled "Neurological disorders" and consisted of four pages (701 words). Subject and difficulty level were representative of the other study materials used by the students. The subject matter built on the subject matter from previous lessons. In the text, for every disorder four different themes (aspects) were distinguished:

- name or description of the neurological disorder;
- origin of the neurological disorder;
- symptoms of the neurological disorder;
- treatment of the neurological disorder.

In the experimental colour condition, the parts of the text which correspond to these themes had background colours. Each theme had its own colour: red for name, blue for origin, green for symptoms and grey for treatment. At the top of every page the meanings of the colours were explained.

The colours were realized with a colour copier. They were printed with 50 dots per inch and a density of 10%. This resulted in light background colours in order to maximize the contrast with the black characters of the text.

Apart from the use of colour, the text in the colour condition and the text in the black-and-white condition showed no differences. Both had the same layout: paragraph titles, numbering of sections, and blank line spaces between the parts which differed with respect to the above mentioned themes. Also, the content was exactly the same.

Possibly unclear elements and other possible flaws in the text had been located in a pilot study. It appeared that the first version of the text was too long to be used in one lesson period (2x50 minutes) together with a test and a questionnaire. The final four-page version of the instructional text was drawn up on the basis of the results of the pilot study.

Recall measurement

An open answer test was used to assess what text information was recalled by the students after studying the text. The test consisted of 28 knowledge and comprehension questions about facts and concepts from the text. The test was composed using a test matrix, in order to spread the questions proportionally over the text. The questions were pilot-tested together with the text. The test was administered twice: one quarter of an hour after studying the text and after one week. The second time, the questions were put in a different order.

The test was scored by two independent judges. Correct answers were rated 1 to 4 points, depending on the difficulty and the scope of the question. The maximum score was 48 points. The inter-judge reliability was computed by correlating all pairs of total scores for each student. This was done for the first and second test separately, yielding correlations of .94 and .96 respectively. In cases where individual questions were scored differently, a third judge decided on the score.

Measurement of the valuation of studying the text

To measure students' valuation of studying the text, a questionnaire with five-point scale items was developed. In addition to items which were identical for both conditions (colour or black-and-white), a few condition-specific items were incorporated in the questionnaire. The valuation items were added to the questionnaire about background information (previous schooling, study results and sex). The text of these items is printed in the section on results.

Measurement of student variables

Two student variables, verbal intelligence and cognitive style (field dependence/independence), were assessed. Because of the structuring function of the colour, it seemed desirable to plan some further analysis, to look for possible relations between these student variables and the effects of using colour in instructional texts. In order to get an indication of verbal intelligence in a relatively short testing time, the sub-test "Analogies" of the "Differential Ability Test" (DAT) was used (Fokkema & Dirkzwager, 1961). Field (in)dependence was measured using the "Group Embedded Figures Test" (Oltman, Raskin & Witkin, 1971).

Procedure

The students took part in two sessions:
- In the first session the instructional text was studied, the questionnaire with background and valuation questions was filled out, and the open answer test was administered.
- In the second session, which took place one week after the first one, the open answer test was administered once more. Next, the Group Embedded Figures Test and the Analogies Test were administered.

Before studying the text, the students were instructed to study the text thoroughly "to become familiar with the main points, but also to remember the most important details". They were not allowed to underline or make notes in the text (because of the chance that the control group would do this more often than the experimental group, which might influence the results). The students were told that after studying the text, an open answer test would be administered. Study time was limited to a maximum of 45 minutes. All students finished within this time. As soon as a subject stopped studying the text, his or her time was written down (in minutes). The students were not told that they would get the open answer test a second time during the follow-up session, one week later.

RESULTS

Equivalency of the experimental and the control group

It was ascertained whether the randomly composed groups could be considered equivalent with respect to sex, previous schooling, study results, cognitive style and verbal intelligence. From Table 1 it is clear that no significant differences occurred on these variables.

Table 1
Equivalency of experimental (colour) and control group (black-and-white)

Sex (n)	male	female	$\chi^2(1)$	p			
Colour	10	36	0.01	.96			
Black-White	10	37					

Previous schooling(n)*	havo	vwo	mbo	vhbo	others	$\chi^2(4)$	p
Colour	31	9	1	0	5	3.49	.48
Black-White	27	13	3	1	3		

Study results(scores)**	n	M	SD	t	p
Anatomy and physiology					
Colour	45	1.20	0.55	0.04	.97
Black-White	47	1.19	0.40	(df=91)	
Hygienics					
Colour	45	0.80	0.70	-0.74	.46
Black-White	46	0.94	0.74	(df=89)	
Nursing					
Colour	46	0.93	0.54	-1.34	.18
Black-White	47	1.09	0.55	(df=91)	
Sociology					
Colour	41	0.95	0.64	-0.03	.97
Black-White	45	0.96	0.56	(df=84)	
Psychology					
Colour	46	1.11	0.49	-0.37	.71
Black-White	47	1.17	0.52	(df=91)	
Philosophy					
Colour	43	1.79	0.42	-1.03	.31
Black-White	47	1.88	0.34	(df=88)	

Cognitive style (Group Embedded Figures Test)	n	M	SD	t	p
Colour	46	14.00	3.71	1.62	.11
Black-White	47	12.62	4.46	(df=91)	

Verbal intelligence (Analogies Test)	n	M	SD	t	p
Colour	46	35.43	6.39	1.36	.18
Black-White	47	33.62	6.54	(df=91)	

*   havo = higher secondary education (comparable to secondary modern school level)
      vwo = pre-university secondary education
      mbo = intermediate vocational education
      vhbo = preparatory vocational education
**   A fail mark=0, a pass mark= 1, a good mark= 2.
      Not everyone followed all courses

Primary analysis

Recall of contents
Using t-tests, it was determined whether there were differences between the colour condition and the black-and-white condition with respect to the recall of contents immediately after the learning session and one week after (Table 2).

Table 2
Recall of contents for immediate and delayed testing

	n	M	SD	t(91)	p
		Immediate testing			
Colour	46	29.46	6.51	-1.72	.09
Black-White	47	31.66	5.81		
		Delayed testing			
Colour	46	22.78	7.53	-0.84	.40
Black-White	47	24.00	6.39		

Neither immediate testing nor delayed testing showed significant differences between the two groups.

Valuation of studying the text
It was analysed whether students in the colour condition valued the studying of the text differently from students in the black-and-white condition. This was done applying t-tests to those valuation items which were identical in both conditions.

Table 3 shows that students who studied the coloured text considered it significantly less disturbing that they were not allowed to underline parts of the text than students in the black-and-white condition (the sixth question; $p <$ .05, two-tailed). If one allows for one-tailed testing, which is possible given the formulated expectation, the difference between the conditions is significant also for the second question ($p = .035$, one-tailed): students with a coloured text thought the studying of the text to be significantly easier than students with a black-and-white text.

To find out how the students appreciated the use of colour in the experimental condition, some extra questions were added to the questionnaire. These questions and the answers are shown in Table 4. It appears that by and large, the students value the addition of colour positively.

Table 3
Valuation of studying the text in the colour and the black-and-white condition

	n	M	SD	t	p
I thought studying the text					
very tiresome (1) - very pleasant (5)					
Colour	45	3.07	1.03	-0.78	.44
Black-White	45	3.22	0.85	(df=88)	
I thought studying the text					
very difficult (1) - very easy (5)					
Colour	42	3.43	0.77	1.84	.07
Black-White	46	3.13	0.75	(df=86)	
I thought the contents of the text					
very dull (1) - very interesting (5)					
Colour	46	3.57	0.94	-0.98	.33
Black-White	47	3.74	0.82	(df=91)	
Previously I was not at all interested					
(1) - very interested (5)					
in taking part in the investigation					
Colour	46	2.63	0.93	-0.16	.88
Black-White	47	2.66	0.87	(df=91)	
During the investigation I was not at					
all interested (1) - very interested (5)					
in taking part					
Colour	46	2.96	0.82	-0.50	.62
Black-White	47	3.04	0.86	(df=91)	
I thought it very disturbing (1) -					
not at all disturbing (5), that					
I was not allowed to underline					
in the text while studying					
Colour	46	3.67	1.43	3.16	.002
Black-White	47	2.77	1.34	(df=91)	
I thought it very disturbing (1) -					
not at all disturbing (5), that					
I was not allowed to take notes					
while studying					
Colour	46	3.15	1.52	1.53	.13
Black-White	47	2.66	1.59	(df=91)	

Further analyses

In addition to the primary analysis just described, some further analyses were carried out on the data obtained.

Study time
The time used to study the text was recorded for every single student. The mean study time in the colour condition did not differ significantly from the

Table 4
Valuation of the use of colour in the study text

	M	SD
That the study text had been printed in coloured paragraphs, I thought:		
very nice (1) - very annoying (5)	2.18	0.96
very handy (1) - very difficult (5)	1.85	0.87
very clarifying (1) - very confusing (5)	2.07	0.84
very necessary (1) - very redundant (5)	3.07	0.89
Owing to the colours in the study text, I probably have the text:		
better understood (1) - worse understood (5)	2.59	0.62
better remembered (1) - worse remembered (5)	2.39	0.71
If parts in my text books have been coloured, I thought it:		
very nice (1) - very annoying (5)	2.26	0.71
very handy (1) - very difficult (5)	1.98	0.80
very clarifying (1) - very confusing (5)	2.09	0.77
very necessary (1) - very redundant (5)	3.02	0.75
I could distinguish the colours in the study text:		
very well (1) - very bad (5)	1.26	0.71

mean in the black-and-white condition: $M_{black-and-white}= 39.38$, $M_{colour}= 39.18$, $t(91)= -0.17$, $p= .87$.

Cognitive style, verbal intelligence and study results
Because it was possible that cognitive style, verbal intelligence or study results had influenced the effects of the conditions differently, a further analysis was carried out. Field-dependent students, students of low verbal intelligence and students with poor study results might possibly benefit from the colour-imposed structure of the experimental text. Field-independent students, students of high verbal intelligence and students with good study results might do better with a black-and- white text, because colour structuring might interfere with the need of these students to structure information themselves. For each of these three variables, students were assigned to groups with high and low scores using the median split technique. Table 5 shows the means of these groups per condition.

A 2x2 analysis of variance yielded no significant interactions between condition and the variables under study. An effect that did occur across conditions was that students of high verbal intelligence and with good study results scored significantly higher on the immediate test than students of low verbal intelligence and with poor study results: $F(1,91)_{verb.int.}= 4.71$, $p= .03$; $F(1,91)_{study res.}= 6.37$, $p= .01$. On the delayed test, field-independent

Table 5
Means per condition of groups with high and low values of cognitive style, verbal intelligence and study results

	Week 1		Week 2	
	Colour	Black-white	Colour	Black-white
Field dependent (n=45)	27.79	30.73	21.16	22.23
Field independent (n=48)	30.63	32.81	23.93	26.19
Low verbal (n=49)	27.40	30.93	20.90	23.24
High verbal (n=44)	31.00	32.83	24.08	25.22
Low study results (n=50)	27.64	30.56	21.88	22.92
High study results (n=43)	31.62	32.91	23.86	25.23

students scored significantly higher than did the field-dependent students: $F(1,91)= 5.55$, $p= .02$.

DISCUSSION AND CONCLUSION

Main results

The main results may be summarized as follows:
- No significant differences were found with respect to recall of parts of the text between the colour and the black-and-white condition. This holds for the immediate as well as for the delayed test.
- With respect to valuation of studying the text, students in the colour condition considered it less disturbing that they were not allowed to underline parts of the text than did students in the black-and-white condition. Also, studying the text was thought to be easier in the colour condition than in the black-and-white condition. The use of colour was experienced as convenient and clarifying.
- Studying the coloured text did not take more time than studying the black-and-white text.
- No significant interactions were found between recall and the student variables cognitive style, verbal intelligence and study results.

Discussion

There may be various explanations for the result of this study, that the use of colour to structure an instructional text did not yield extra recall of the contents of the text.

The result may be attributed to a phenomenon described by Salomon (1984): if tasks are perceived as more difficult, students tend to invest more mental effort, which causes them to learn more. This phenomenon may have played a part in the black-and-white condition, because of the fact that the students in this condition considered the text significantly more difficult than did the students in the colour condition. Also, students in the black-and-white condition thought it to be more disturbing that they were not allowed to underline parts of the text than did students in the colour condition. They obviously felt more need to structure the text further. Because of the perceived task difficulty, the students in the black-and-white condition may have invested more mental effort than students in the colour condition. Owing to this, they yielded, contrary to our expectations, the same results as those in the colour condition.

Another possible explanation of the obtained result is that students in the colour condition did not pay attention to the colour while studying the text. For this reason the coloured structure cues did not yield extra effects on the storage and recall of the hierarchically lower ordered facts and concepts.

To increase attention for the colour cues, it may have been better not only to explain the function of each colour on top of each page, but also to instruct the students about it orally or to give them the opportunity to exercise with another coloured text beforehand. This was impossible, however, given the constraints of the experimental situation: the experimental group and the control group were sitting in the same room. In retrospect, it may have been advisable to ask students in the colour condition after they studied the text, whether they knew the functions of the colour in the text.

The result of this study, that the students evaluated the use of colour positively, calls for special mention. In the opinion of the students the study of the text became easier owing to the colour structuring; they experienced it as an aid in studying. However, the colour structuring had no effects on the recall of the text contents. This is a contradictory result that has been found more often in colour research (Lamberski, 1980; Vroemen, 1986). One may wonder if the positive evaluation of the colour by the students has some other influence on the study activities. Is there an influence on the motivation and concentration while studying, or on the attitude towards the text contents? Can students longer sustain studying coloured texts? Several of these questions have been asked more than once (Lamberski, 1980) in colour research. To our knowledge, they have not been worked out and investigated in the research on colour use in verbal contexts.

One may wonder whether the same non-significant results would have been found with other subjects and other instructional texts.
- The research on the use of colour in verbal contexts, which was described by Lamberski (1980), deals mainly with students from primary school.

Young children may be more sensitive to coloured directions than older students are.
-   The instructional text used in the experiment was well structured in both conditions, by way of section headings, subdivisions and blank line spacing. It is possible that the text structure, without colour use, was clear enough for the students. They may not need the extra colour directions. However, for practical reasons this research design had been explicitly chosen. For, if one strives for text books which are as cheap as possible to the consumer, the more expensive colour printing is only then justified if the recall effects of colour are positive in comparison with a well structured, cheaper, black-and-white text.

From the preceding section it will be clear, that broad generalizations are not possible on the basis of this study. Moreover, the study was limited to the effects of colour on the recall of text parts. The use of colour to structure a text may, however, facilitate the searching for, and location of information in the text (see for instance Stoverinck, 1982). This will be examined in follow-up research. In this research the effects of colour used to focus attention to main parts of a text (rather than to structure a text) will also be investigated. In that case the colour use will be used as an instructional design variable to emphasize critical aspects of the subject matter (Merrill, 1983). Because of the possible explanations of the results of this study, it is advisable as well to gather data on study activities and mental effort in further research on the use of colour in designing instructional texts.

Nevertheless, if one intends to use colour as a means to structure instructional texts, it seems recommendable as yet not to ignore the results of this study completely. The observed absence of recall effects may then be weighted against the positive valuation of the use of colour, at the same time considering the implications of the extra cost of colour printing.

REFERENCES

Carter, M.C., & Cahill, R.C. (1976). Color code size for searching displays of different density. *Human Factors, 18*(3), 273-280.

De Weert, Ch.M.M. (1984). Veridical perception: A key to the choise of colours and brightnesses in multicolour displays. In P. Gibson (Ed.), *Monochrome versus colour in electronic displays.* Farnbourough, RAE, 181-188.

Fokkema, S.D., & Dirkzwager, A. (1961). *Handleiding bij het gebruik van de Differentiële Aanleg Test* [Differential Aptitude Test: User's guide]. Amsterdam: Swets & Zeitlinger.

Hartley, J. (1978). *Designing instructional text.* London: Kogan Page.

Jonassen, D.H. (1982). *The technology of text: Principles for structuring, designing, and displaying text.* Englewood Cliffs, NJ: Educational Technology.

Jonassen, D.H. (1985). *The technology of text: Vol.2. Principles for structuring, designing, and displaying text.* Englewood Cliffs, NJ: Educational Technology.

Kerstjens, W. (1988). *Kleur in instructiemateriaal* [Colour in instructional materials]. Enschede: Universiteit Twente, Faculteit Toegepaste Onderwijskunde.

Kulhavy, R.W., Schmid, R.F., & Walker, C.H. (1977). Temporal organization in prose. *American Educational Research Journal, 14*, 115-123.

Lamberski, R.J. (1980). *A comprehensive and critical review of the methodology and findings in color investigations.* Paper presented at the Annual Convention of the Association for Educational Communications and Technology in Denver.

Lucas, D.D., & Di Vesta, F.J. (1980). Learner-generated organizational aids: Effects on learning from text. *Journal of Educational Psychology, 72*, 304-311.

Merrill, M.D. (1983). Component display theory. In C.M. Reigeluth (Ed.), *Instructional-design theories and models: An overview of their current status* (pp. 279-333). Hillsdale, NJ: Lawrence Erlbaum.

Oltman, P.K., Raskin, E., & Witkin, H.A. (1971). *Group Embedded Figures Test.* Palo Alto, CA: Consulting Psychologists.

Reigeluth, C.M., & Stein, F.S. (1983). The elaboration theory of instruction. In C.M. Reigeluth (Ed.), *Instructional-design theories and models: An overview of their current status* (pp. 335-381). Hillsdale, NJ: Lawrence Erlbaum.

Reising, J.M., & Emerson, T.J. (1985). *Colour in quantitative and qualitative display formats: Does colour help?* International Conference on Colour in Information Technology and Visual Displays, 1-5.

Salomon, G. (1984). Television is "easy" and print is "tough": The differential investment of mental effort in learning as a function of perception and attributions. *Journal of Educational Psychology, 76*(4), 647-658.

Shimmerlik, S.M. (1978). Organization theory and memory for prose. *Review of Educational Research, 48*, 103-120.

Stoverinck, T. (1982). *The use of colour coding on visual display units.* Utrecht: Universiteit van Utrecht, Psychologisch Laboratorium.

Van Hout Wolters, B. (1986). *Markeren van kerngedeelten in studieteksten: Een proces-produkt benadering* [Cueing of key phrases in instructional texts: A process-product approach]. Lisse: Swets & Zeitlinger.

Vroemen, M.W. (1986). *Colour in CRT-display design: Lay-out and coding.* Utrecht: Universiteit van Utrecht, Psychologisch Laboratorium.

6

THE ROLE OF AN ADVANCE ORGANIZER ON CNC-PROGRAM DEBUGGING PERFORMANCE

Georg G.H. Rakers
Nederlandse Philips Bedrijven B.V., Corporate Industrial Design
Jules M. Pieters
Sanne Dijkstra
University of Twente

ABSTRACT

This chapter sketches a theory of how human subjects program computer numerical controlled (CNC) machine tools and reports an experiment on the role of an advance organizer on CNC program debugging performance[1].

INTRODUCTION

Designing and developing the human factors aspect in computing systems has in the past decade become one of the main topics of interest in the cognitive and computer sciences. Typical research issues were computer programming, program debugging, human factors in data organization and access, man-machine-interaction and user interface design.

Although a massive body of research on computer programming exists (e.g. Adelson, 1981, 1984; Mayer, 1975, 1976a, 1981; Shneiderman, 1976, 1980; Wiedenbeck, 1985), to our knowledge hardly any experimental work has yet addressed programming performance within automated manufacturing system environments. The introduction of information technology such as computer numerical controlled (CNC) machine tools onto the shopfloor of manufacturing industry, and, as a consequence, in vocational education, has created however a new domain of interest and instructional research (Kemp & Clegg, 1987; Pritschow & Viefhaus, 1987; Rakers, 1987; Rakers, Pieters & de Bruijn, 1988; Weule, Löffler & Selinger, 1987). Compared to traditional manual machine tools these new computerized manufacturing systems require programming, proving-out and editing (e.g. debugging). This means that the introduction of information technology onto the shopfloor demands new, cognitive skills (cf. Rakers, 1987; Rakers et al, 1988). Teaching and training these new cognitive skills however requires the design of new instructional systems.

CNC machines are fully computerized manufacturing systems suitable for (interactive) shop floor programming. In contouring systems the cutting tool is moved along the axes (e.g. lathes). In point-to-point systems the workpiece is moved along the axes (e.g. drilling and milling machines). The experiment described in this chapter concerns a CNC lathe. In contouring systems like a CNC lathe only two axes are required to command the motions of the tool. Since the spindle is horizontal, lathes (or turning machines) have one horizontal axis (denoted by "Z"), and one cross axis (denoted by "X"), being horizontal as well.

Programming CNC machines is assumed to be solving a technical problem in two knowledge domains (Rakers, 1987; Rakers et al, 1988). First, the operator has to solve the problem of which steps should be carried out one after another in the process of manufacturing the workpiece. Second, the operator has to write a CNC computer program that will actually perform the sequence of operations on a visible object.

To program CNC machines therefore means to apply two kinds of knowledge, (a) of the designed workpiece, and (b) of the CNC programming language. This means that for programming CNC machines two aspects are involved: A concrete, *spatial* aspect and an abstract, *verbal* or textual, programming aspect.

It can be hypothesized that these two on the surface apparently different aspects will have consequences for the operator's mental model of the manufacturing of a workpiece. It can further be hypothesized that both aspects, because of these consequences, also will have an important impact on the vocational education of the CNC machine operator, and therefore on the design of the instructional system. So it is crucial to understand the role of these two aspects and to gain knowledge about how these aspects can be influenced by instructional manipulation techniques.

Studies of how human subjects interact with computer systems have shown that the benefit of having an adequate mental model of the workings of a computerized device lies in the fact that within the context of learning specific procedures the mental model enables users to infer exactly how the device should be operated, given a certain task (Kieras, 1987; Kieras & Bovair, 1984).

Program structure, meaningfulness and chunking of new information into meaningful sets is important for learning a computer language and how to program. Mayer (1975, 1976a, 1976b, 1979, 1981) used advance organizers as an instructional technique to increase the novice's understanding of computers and computer programming. Mayer provided evidence that novices' understanding of the computer system and programming performance significantly increases if (a) the way of data processing of the computer system is explained by using a concrete model of the computer and (b) learners are encouraged to actively put new technical information into their own words by comparisons and analogies. A concrete model of the computer and verbal elaborations act as advance organizers to which new information can be assimilated.

The advance organizer is assumed to act as an assimilative context of either verbal or visual information to which new technical information can be assimilated. The advance organizer is meant to influence the learner's encoding process and is therefore presented prior to learning a larger body of new technical information.

Testing the role of an advance organizer on CNC program debugging performance was the purpose of this study.

METHOD

Subjects

Thirty-nine undergraduate students in mechanical engineering of the University of Twente participated in this experiment. They were all freshmen who had just completed a first year course in production technology. The experiment took place on the last day of their course. The subjects were not paid, but participated to fulfill course requirements.

Task

The subjects' task was to check, debug and correct a CNC computer program for a lathe.

Materials

The test material concerned a short pretest and a booklet containing a short, one page, instruction about what kind of task the Ss had to accomplish, an engineering drawing of a piece of chess (Queen), information about what kind of and how many tools the Ss could use (one page), a list of specific program functions and their definitions (one page), and the bugged CNC program for the manufacturing of the Queen. The program had three types of bugs in it, (1) bugs referring to grammatical errors (Knowing What); (2) bugs within a procedure or program function (Knowing How); and (3) bugs in the composition of procedures or program functions, i.e. the program indeed realizes the goal, but it took more steps, statements or procedures (Knowing When).

Procedure

Subjects where randomly assigned to the control (= No Advance Advice) group or the experimental (= Advance Advice) group. All Ss had first to complete the pretest. The pretest tested their CNC programming knowledge, and included twelve questions about their declarative knowledge (*Knowing What*), and eight questions about their procedural knowledge (*Knowing How*). The pretest took about ten minutes. Immediately after the pretest Ss started with their debugging task. Because of being a so called "manual programming" task, the experiment could be designed as a paper and pencil test. All Ss received the same task material. Only the Ss in the experimental group also received advance advice. This written advance advice was formulated in goal statements (cf. Sebrechts & Deck, 1986), and told the Ss in the experimental group how they should accomplish their task. These goal statements were: write a complete program, write an efficient program, and avoid unnecessary changes of chisel and carriage.

RESULTS

The results of the pretest showed no differences between the two groups. This means that the Ss came from the same population and had the same amount of CNC programming knowledge.

Table 1 shows the results of our experiment. As can be seen, no significant difference between the two groups were found in neither of the three types of bugs.

DISCUSSION

The results of our experiment on the role of advance advice as an advance organizer on CNC computer program debugging performance do not support the hypothesis that an advance organizer assists novices in debugging a CNC program. Advance organizers are supposed to be ineffective: (a) if the subjects under study are high ability subjects (Mayer, 1975), (b) if the learners have already their own models or concepts (Bury, Boyle, Evey & Neal, 1982; Mayer, 1976a), (c) if the advance organizer contains specific content from the to be learned information (Mayer, 1979), and (d) if after receiving the advance organizer there is unstructured access to the training materials (Sebrechts & Deck, 1986). The subjects in this experiment were no expert performers, so they did not have any model of their own. This leaves explanation three or four. Explanation four is most probable, because our subjects were all freshmen with hardly any real hands-on experience with manufacturing. They did not have the right model or representation in which the advance planning information could be placed.

Table 1
Mean number of expected and observed bugs for three types of bugs

Type of Bug	X Expected	X Observed		Significance
		AA	NA	
KNOWING WHAT				
Change	12	2.0	2.1	NS
KNOWING HOW				
Change	13	2.2	1.7	NS
Delete	2	0.5	0.7	NS
Insert	4	0.4	0.3	NS
KNOWING WHEN				
Change	1	0.1	0.1	NS
Delete	7 (6)	1.2	1.3	NS
Insert	3	0.3	0.4	NS
Move	2 (3)	0.1	0.1	NS
Number of Programlines	55	21.4	24.2	NS
Number of Functional Units ("chunks")	13	3.7	4.8	NS

What do these results mean for teaching CNC program debugging skills in particular and the design of the instructional system for the vocational education of the CNC programmer in general?

The suggestion of Dalbey and Linn (1985) that programming instructions should focus on higher cognitive activities, such as planning and debugging, is not supported in this study on CNC programming. Our findings give us a reason to suggest that for teaching CNC programming skills a graphical real-time simulation of the manufacturing process can be a powerful educational tool to shortcut the elaborative learning of expert strategies for program debugging. *What you see is what you did.* When both an animated representation of the blank and the cutting tool and the textual representation of the CNC program are displayed on the same screen, the comparison of the program with the current manufacturing stage can be made directly and the bug spotted immediately.

For the design of the instructional system we would suggest that CNC programming instructions with regard to debugging should concentrate on planning (*Knowing When*). Teach CNC programmers problem solving skills which concern program efficiency, mapping out the steps to take in the manufacturing process, etc. (thus, skills for debugging the program *plan*). In practice, this would mean teaching CNC programmers the cognitive skills and strategies that experts find natural to use as soon as possible, i.e. top-down, and reasoning from an abstract hierarchical programming knowledge representation.

Adequately designed computerized instruction can offer all the advantages conventional apprenticeship once had. It only brings its benefits in different ways. A well designed instructional system nowadays can in its simplest form be incorporated into the HELP-facility of an application program, can be a functional part of the user-interface throughout the software system, or might come as an intelligent tutoring system, separated from the application program. Our findings suggest that (a) an instructional system for CNC programming, either by way of a course or by means of an intelligent tutoring system, should be designed around solving the problem of planning (e.g. *sequence control*). Thus, focussing on Knowing When (and where and why) the steps in the manufacturing process should be executed (*criterion knowledge*). Our findings also suggest (b) that the user-interface of a CNC machine tool's control system should be designed to display on the same screen both the concrete pictorial information of the manufacturing process and the abstract textual information of the CNC program. Furthermore, (c) that a HELP-facility incorporated into the user-interface of the control system should support the CNC machine tool user on the level of the higher cognitive activity of planning the most efficient machining sequences.

Note

1.   The authors wish to express their gratitude to Fred Brigham and Ian McClelland for their helpful comments on a draft of this chapter.

REFERENCES

Adelson, B. (1981). Problem solving and the development of abstract categories in programming languages. *Memory & Cognition*, *9*(4), 422-433.

Adelson, B. (1984). When novices surpass experts: The difficulty of a task may increase with expertise. *Journal of Experimental Psychology: Learning, Memory, and Cognition*, *10*(3), 483-495.

Bury, K.F., Boyle, J.M., Evey, R.J., & Neal, A.S. (1982). Windowing versus scrolling on a visual display terminal. *Human Factors*, *24*(4), 385-394.

Dalbey, J., & Linn, M.C. (1985). The demands and requirements of computer programming: A literature review. *Journal of Educational Computing Research*, *1*(3), 253-274.

Kemp, N.J., & Clegg, C.W. (1987). Information technology and job design: A case study on computerized numerically controlled machine tool working. *Behaviour and Information Technology, 6*(2), 109-124.

Kieras, D.E. (1987). *What mental model should be taught: Choosing instructional content for complex engineered systems* (Technical Report No. 24). Ann Arbor: University of Michigan.

Kieras, D.E., & Bovair, S. (1984). The role of a mental model in learning to operate a device. *Cognitive Science, 8,* 255-273.

Mayer, R.E. (1975). Different problem-solving competencies established in learning computer programming with and without meaningful models. *Journal of Educational Psychology, 67*(6), 725-734.

Mayer, R.E. (1976a). Some conditions of meaningful learning for computer programming: Advance organizers and subject control of frame order. *Journal of Educational Psychology, 68*(2), 143-150.

Mayer, R.E. (1976b). Comprehension as affected by structure problem representation. *Memory & Cognition, 4*(3), 249-255.

Mayer, R.E. (1979). Can advance organizers influence meaningful learning? *Review of Educational Research, 49*(2), 371-383.

Mayer, R.E. (1981). The psychology of how novices learn computer programming. *Computing Surveys, 13*(1), 121-141.

Pritschow, G., & Viefhaus, R. (1987). Workshop programming of numerical controls. In H.-J. Bullinger and B. Shackel (Eds.), *Human-Computer Interaction - INTERACT '87.* Amsterdam: Elsevier Science Publishers B.V.

Rakers, G.G.H. (1987). *The theory of "Frame of Mind"* (IST-MEMO-87-01). Enschede: Universiteit Twente, Faculteit Toegepaste Onderwijskunde.

Rakers, G.G.H., Pieters, J.M., & de Bruijn, I. (1988). Het leren programmeren van computergestuurde gereedschapwerktuigen: Een afbeeldings-theorie en een informatieverwerkingsmodel. *Tijdschrift voor Onderwijsresearch, 13*(4), 181-200.

Sebrechts, M.M., & Deck, J.G. (1986). Techniques for acquiring computer procedures: Some restrictions on "interaction". In *Proceedings of the Human Factors Society - 30th Annual Meeting - 1986* (pp. 275- 279).

Shneiderman, B. (1976). Exploratory experiments in programmer behavior. *International Journal of Computer and Information Sciences, 5*(2), 123-143.

Weule, H., Löffler, L., & Selinger, Th. (1987). Factory workers and the language barrier. Making computers a tool rather than a nuisance. In H.-J. Bullinger and B. Shackel (Eds.), *Human-Computer Interaction INTERACT '87.* Amsterdam: Elsevier Science Publishers B.V.

Wiedenbeck, S. (1985). Novice/Expert differences in programming skills. *International Journal of Man-Machine Studies, 23,* 383-390.

7

COMPUTER-BASED ENHANCEMENTS FOR THE IMPROVEMENT OF LEARNING

Robert D. Tennyson
University of Minnesota

ABSTRACT

In this chapter I have presented a means by which educators can determine if specific media variables and methods may improve learning. Thus, I did not attempt to debate whether or not media improves learning. Media is but one component in a complex instructional system. A system that involves principles of instructional design as well as methods of instructional delivery. What I have shown here is that to assume that given instructional methods improve learning, those methods must have two aspects. First, they must exhibit a direct trace to a specific learning process. And, second, they must have empirical support that demonstrates their significance.

Because of the purpose of this book to focus on specific topics, I have limited my example of the tracing process to my research findings. That of course limits the generalization of the answer to the question on the effect of media on learning, but I am sure others who have done basic research in instructional technology could make a similar effort. By doing so, there would be additional support for understanding the role of media in improving learning.

INTRODUCTION

For the past 20 years a major debate in the field of educational technology has been the two part question: "does media improve learning?", and if so, "by how much?" Early on, proponents of an affirmative answer based their opinions solely on technocratic assumptions (e.g., Briggs, 1959). This group is still alive today but with increased support from the hard technologists (i.e., computer scientists) which offer such "new" technologies as microworlds, "intelligent" computer-assisted instruction (ICAI), and expert systems. Those educators who answered with a negative, based their conclusions basically on methodogical grounds. They argued first that research findings in favor of the question were flawed in both experimental design and methodology. Given the academic approach to their criticism, the opponents only achieved recognition in a limited circle of educationally based research programs. And, with the rapid development of computer technology following the application of the micro-chip in the later 1970s, the questions no longer seemed relevant. That is, it was assumed to have been answered in the affirmative by the advancement of technology.

However, by the mid-80's, educators by increasing numbers began to realize that maybe the question needed to be reconsidered given the apparent decline in computer popularity as the solution to the crisis in education (Benjamin, 1988). Once again though, the technologists have been successful in fending off the opponents because of several hardware (e.g., interactive video) and software (e.g., LOGO) developments. But, as the new technological "solutions" continue to fail or to be replaced by yet another educational panacea, opponents are still raising the question anew. And as the new technologies become even more sophisticated, the question is actually becoming more important.

The purpose of this chapter is not an answer to the question, but to elaborate on the question and to offer a view that is at the same time a yes and a no. The problem seems not to be the technology, but the failure of proponents to adequately trace the variables of their respective media techniques to clearly defined learning processes. For example, LOGO is supposed to improve thinking skills simply because the student is engaging in a technology-based discovery system. Although proponents of LOGO claim some foundation in neo-Piagetian learning theory, they, for the most part, have invented a set of terms beyond the scope of Piaget's theory which focuses on experience and effort in learning. Piaget emphasized active engagement in the domains of information, not artificial environments divorced from real knowledge.

To illustrate this concept of tracing media-based variables to the improvement of learning, I will concentrate on the program of research that my colleagues and I have been working on since 1971. There are of course other researchers and centres of programmatic research which further illustrate this concept of media research founded in learning theory: for example, Joseph Scandura, Robert Glaser, David Merrill, Paul Merrill, Richard Clark, Steve Ross, and Gavriel Salomon.

TRACING MODEL

In this chapter I will discuss six basic educational components necessary to trace media variables directly to specific learning processes. Because of the focus of my research on computer-based variables, I will not include other media forms (e.g., video and print). The purpose of this chapter is not to explain in detail all of the components, but to propose that an answer to the question on media and improved learning can be done in part by showing the direct linkage of media variables to specific learning conditions and processes.

Information processing model of learning

In my research program, the basic learning theory is directly related to an information processing model. This model has been defined in several sources (Tennyson, 1988; Tennyson & Breuer, 1984; Tennyson & Christensen, 1988). The model includes these system components: (a) the receptor component by which external information is entered into the brain; (b) the perception component where the information is filtered according to individual criteria; (c) the short-term/working memory component which has a dual function. The short-term memory deals only with information at the given moment and does so with no cognitive effort for encoding. Working-memory on the other hand engages directly with long-term memory to encode information into the current knowledge base; (d) the long-term memory component which consists of the storage and retrieval systems. The storage system codes information according to specific types of knowledge (i.e., declarative, procedural, and contextual) while the retrieval system involves the thinking strategies associated with differentiation and integration; and (e) the cognitive process of creating knowledge within the cognitive system itself.

Components of Tracing Model

Table 1 shows the six main components usually associated with the instructional design (ID) process. In practice, however, the links between the components are neither well established operationally or theoretically. My purpose here is to both illustrate and discuss the linkages to propose that media can improve learning when it is viewed as an integral component of the entire ID process.

The six components are:
- Learning Processes. The focus here is on the long-term memory systems of *storage* and *retrieval*. Storage system refers to the learning processes associated with knowledge acquisition (i.e., the encoding and coding of information) while retrieval system refers to the strategies of thinking (i.e., recall, problem solving, and creativity).
- Learning Objectives. The purpose of education is to improve student learning (i.e., knowledge acquisition and employment). Objectives are necessary to identify the type of learning that is desired. The objectives should be linked to specify learning processes.

Table 1
Tracing learning processes to computer-based enhancements

Learning Processes (Long-Term Memory)	Learning Objectives	Knowledge Base	Instructional Variables	Instructional Strategies	Computer-Based Enhancements CONVENTIONAL (branching)	INTELLIGENT (rule-based)
STORAGE SYSTEM:						
Declarative Knowledge (knowing that)	Verbal/visual Information (awareness and understanding of concepts, rules, & principles)	Schema Characteristics (content: objects, events, & situations)	Label, Definition, Best example, Refreshment, Expository Examples	Drill & Practice (e.g., rhearsal, repetition), Lecture	Replacement Ratio, Worked Examples, Graphics	Embedded Refreshment & Remediation, Mixed Initiative Advisement
Procedural Knowledge (knowing how)	Intellectual Skills (ability to employ concepts, rules & principles)	Schema Structure (context organization: algorithm or heuristic)	Interrogatory, Examples (divergent), Attribute Elaboration	Tutorial (e.g., PI, CAI, ICAI, peer tutor)	Format of Examples	Amount of Information, Learning Time, Corrective Error Analysis, Sequence of Information
Contextual Knowledge (knowing when and why)	Contextual Skills (ability to perceive criteria, values & appropriateness)	Schemata Organizational Accessibility (network associations & executive control)	Context (problem), Advance organizer, Feedback, Strategy Information, Cooperative Learning Group Techniques (heterogeneous)	Problem-oriented Simulations	Adjustment of Variables & Conditions	Process Feedback
RETRIEVAL SYSTEM:						
Differentiate Integrate Create	Cognitive Strategies (Develop strategies recall, problem solving, & creativity)		Cooperative Learning Group (homogeneous)	Complex-problem Simulations, Self-Directed Experience		Elaboration & Extension of Variables & Conditions

- Knowledge Base. Analyzing the information to be learned involves not only the basic content but also the structure of the information as knowledge in memory.
- Instructional Variables. The means of instruction are the variables by which information is communicated to the student. In Table 1, I present those basic variables which have been empirically tested to improve learning. The variables are directly linked to their respective primary learning processes. Certain variables may also have secondary links to other processes.
- Instructional Strategies. The instructional strategies identified here only represent those which I have tested in my research program. And, in most situations, employed computers in some capacity.
- Computer-Based Enhancements. The enhancements listed here are subdivided into categories according to their intelligence in decision making. Conventional computer-based instruction (CBI) programs use branching techniques that are determined in the design stage and are preset in the program. Intelligent CBI are rule-based programs that make decisions at the moment the student is learning: Thus, they adjust moment to moment to individual differences.

Tracing declarative knowledge

In general terms, declarative knowledge means "knowing what." For example, the student knows that underlining keywords will improve recall. The learning objective for this learning process is verbal/visual information. What the student learns is both an awareness and understanding of concepts, rules and principles. For example, the student is aware of certain strategies for recalling of information from text. The knowledge base (KB) in my context employs a schema theory application. With this form of learning, the KB identifies the schema characteristics of the knowledge. Characteristics include the objects, events, and situations of a schema. For example, the student has a schema of underlining keywords of scientific text.

The instructional strategies for improving this learning process include variables directed to information that is specific, and perhaps, finite. The variables label and definition provide the location and connection of information in a KB. When a connection is difficult to establish, the refreshing variable focuses on the need for review of appropriate necessary knowledge. To initialize knowledge, the expository presentation of examples establishes a clear case of the content. This is especially important in the learning of complex rules and principles. Instructional strategies of drill and practice help the learner in acquiring the awareness of specific information with an expository presentation (e.g., a lecture) clarifying the understanding. The conventional computer-based enhancements provide for the optimal pacing and display of information while the intelligent enhancements keep the student directly involved with understanding the information to be learned. For example, the mixed-initiative variable allows the student to ask the system a question. Advisement keeps the students informed of their learning progress and needs.

Tracing procedural knowledge

Procedural knowledge is "knowing how." For example, the student knows how to use the *APA Publication Manual* in the writing of scientific text. The learning objective refers to this process as an intellectual skill, in which the students learn how to employ concepts, rules and principles. The KB here identifies the organizational structure of a given schema. For example, the student knows how to use the heuristics necessary to conduct experiments in educational research. The organization of a schema can take many forms, for example an algorithm or strategy used in searching through a data-based retrieval system.

The primary instructional variables at this level focus on practice of the information in problem or interrogatory situations. Examples should be selected to provide a wide range of applications. Divergent examples allow the students to elaborate on their KB. Tutorial instructional strategies provide a convenient method of interaction between the student and the tutor, be it either a human peer tutor or a computer-based tutor. The basic format is question/answer with the tutor challenging the student to clearly employ knowledge to prevent or eliminate misconceptions.

It is with this instructional strategy that the most dramatic advancements in computer-based instruction have been made in the last ten years. The variables listed in Table 1 are all part of my research program for the MAIS (Minnesota Adaptive Instructional System). The MAIS is a complete intelligent instructional system with an expert tutor monitoring student learning at all levels of learning. Variables monitored by the MAIS include the amount of information, learning time, sequence of information, feedback, and corrective error analysis. In fact, the MAIS implements all of the enhancements listed in Table 1. Additionally, all of the enhancements have been empirically tested in both laboratory and applied environments (Tennyson & Christensen, 1988).

Tracing contextual knowledge

This learning process refers to the acquisition of the knowledge of "when and why." For example, the student knows the value of knowing different types of reading strategies. The learning objective, contextual skills, implies the ability to perceive the criteria, values, and/or appropriateness for employing concepts, rules and principles. The KB represents an analysis of the schematic network associations and the rules which governur the connections. Knowledge in a KB is represented in a variety of ways. For purposes of education, it is often possible to represent this information in a number forms: for example, a taxonomy, a category, or a hierarchy. The KB is structured to represent how the knowledge may be organized in memory. Of importance to the KB is the identification of criteria associated with the structure. For example, the learning objective suggests that the student needs to know the conditions of employment as well as the how of employment.

The instructional variables for this learning process influence student learning in two ways: First, they provide an opportunity for the students to experience the KB; and second, they allow the students an opportunity to develop criteria, values, and appropriateness. Very often these variables are used in all of the identified instructional strategies. The variables of context and advance organizer improve the initial awareness of what is to be learned by helping the student to select and organize appropriate existing knowledge. For example, selecting a specific method or strategy for organizing resources to study. Feedback and strategy information improve the integration of the new knowledge into the KB.

Cooperative learning group techniques improve contextual knowledge acquisition by allowing students to both develop solutions and see alternative solutions to problem situations. Within heterogeneous groups, the students work towards a specific goal by using their respective abilities and aptitudes and, by doing so, improve their understanding of the criteria, values, and appropriateness of knowing when and why to employ knowledge. The problem-oriented simulation allows students to work on situations that replicate the employment of the knowledge they are acquiring. Such employment requires them to make decisions on knowledge selection and organization and, by working in a group, see how their ideas relate to the others. Computer-based simulations can provide ease in adjusting the variables and conditions of situations as well as delivering the simulation.

Tracing retrieval strategies

Most often cognitive theories of learning focus on knowledge acquisition while basically ignoring employment of knowledge in the service of thinking (i.e., recall, problem solving, and creativity). However, the main goal of education is not only the acquisition of knowledge, but also the improvement and employment of knowledge. The traditional schooling paradigm of learning information to develop a disciplined work ethic only indirectly helped students improve their cognitive strategies in thinking. Contemporary cognitive psychology that deals with retrieval system theory indicates that thinking strategies develop most adequately when working concurrently with the KB. That is, thinking strategies in recall, problem solving, and creativity are developed not as general strategies but as specific forms of knowledge embedded in the schemata. And, as strategies, the thinking processes of differentiation, integration and creation can be developed and improved.

Therefore, such cognitive strategy development should be an integral part of the instructional system.

For example, my general recommendations for learning time allocation in a curriculum plan for each learning process is as follows: declarative knowledge, 10%; procedural knowledge, 20%; contextual knowledge, 25%; cognitive strategies, 30%; and creativity, 15%. That is, rather than using almost 100% of the instructional time for the learning objectives of knowledge acquisition, a major part of the time needs to be allocated to thinking strategy development and improvement. The shift from the traditional paradigm of focusing on knowledge acquisition to increased emphasis on thinking strategy development puts learning responsibility, or power, more in the hands of the student. This is accomplished by instructional strategies that employ complex-problem simulations within cooperative learning group techniques.

Complex-problem simulations (Tennyson, Thurlow, & Breuer, 1987) present meaningful and complex problem situations in which students are required to make solution proposals using knowledge stored in memory. The basic format of the simulation is to group students according to similarity of cognitive complexity (i.e., their general skills in differentiation and integration). Within the group, each student is to prepare a proposal individually and then present it to the group. At this point, the student is to advocate his/her proposal. Because of the conflict in this format, each student sees increasingly sophisticated alternatives to the situation which helps them both develop thinking strategies and to elaborate and extend their schemata. Additionally, as the simulated variables and conditions change, the students are faced with situations that require them to create knowledge to make proposals. The computer-based enhancements include both the conventional methods of simulation variables and conditions adjustments as well as intelligent methods of monitoring the progress and needs of each student.

REFERENCES

Benjamin, Jr., L.T. (1988). A history of teaching machines. *American Psychologist, 43*, 703-712.

Briggs, L.J. (1959). Teaching machines for training of military personnel in maintenance of electronic equipment. In E. Galanter (Ed.), *Automatic teaching: The state of the art* (pp. 131-145). New York: Wiley.

Park, O., & Tennyson, R.D. (1984). Computer-based instructional systems for adaptive education: A review. *Review of Contemporary Education, 2*, 121-135.

Park, O., & Tennyson, R.D. (1986). Response-sensitive design strategies for sequence order on concepts and presentation form of examples using computer-based instruction. *Journal of Educational Psychology, 78*, 153-158.

Tennyson, R.D. (1988). An instructional strategy planning model to improve learning and cognition. *Computers in Human Behavior, 4*, 13-22.

Tennyson, R.D., & Breuer, K. (1984). Cognitive-based design guidelines for using video and computer technology in course development. In O. Zuber-Skerrit (Ed.), *Video in higher education* (pp. 26-63). London: Kogan.

Tennyson, R.D., & Christensen, D.L. (1988). MAIS: An intelligent learning system. In D.H. Jonassen (Ed.), *Instructional designs for microcomputer courseware* (pp. 247-274). Hillsdale, NJ: Erlbaum.

Tennyson, R.D., Thurlow, R., & Breuer, K. (1987). Problem-oriented simulations to develop and improve higher-order thinking strategies. *Computers in Human Behavior, 3*, 239-268.

8

DIFFERENTIAL EFFECTS OF PROTOTYPE-BASED INSTRUCTION ON THE FORMATION OF DIAGNOSTIC SKILLS

Jan Gulmans
University of Twente

ABSTRACT

Prototype theory suggests that categorization is facilitated by prior formation of a prototype, i.e. a typical case of a category. In this experiment different prototypes of a medical concept were presented. The differential effects of this prototype-based instruction on the formation of diagnostic skills, using the model of concept learning developed by Merrill and Tennyson (1977), were investigated. The results of the experiment show confirming evidence that learning diagnostic skills has to be organized around a prototypical case of a disease.

INTRODUCTION

A diagnosis is the process of determining the nature of an illness. The outcome of the process is the categorization of the diseased condition. The diagnostic skill is the careful examination of the symptoms or features of the disease. Because a diagnosis implies the categorization of a disease, learning to diagnose is conceived of as concept learning. Thus the instruction for learning to diagnose will be based on an instructional design model for the learning of concepts. Concept learning is the process in which subjects learn to categorize objects, processes or events. After attaining a concept, new, unencountered objects, processes or events, technically labeled as "instances", can be categorized. There are a number of different theories of concept learning. The classical theory was formulated by Bruner, Goodnow and Austin (1955). They assume that the world consists of entities which have fixed attributes and fixed relations between those entities comprised in each instance of a concept. Within the classical theory, defining attributes are those which are necessary and sufficient for deciding if an instance is an example of a category. One of the modern theories of concept learning is prototype theory (Rosch, 1975). Within this theory category membership is determined by the resemblance to the most typical case. This prototype encompasses the most frequently encountered attributes of a category. Merrill and Tennyson (1977) and Tennyson and Cocchiarella (1986) have developed an instructional design model for concept learning, which is based on prototype theory. They assume that concept learning encompasses deductive processes. These processes are based on classification which consists of generalization and discrimination. This design model needs still further confirmation.

Elstein, Shulman and Sprafka (1978) assume that the diagnostic process is based on a hypothetical-deductive strategy. This implies that on the basis of clues a list of potential hypotheses is formulated and that these hypotheses are successively tested until the final diagnosis. A diagnostic decision presupposes knowledge as to the causes, the symptoms and the course of a disease. At the end of the process the diagnostician has to decide which disease is involved. The diagnostic process has both deductive and inductive components. In the case of a valid deduction an inference is made in which the conclusion results logically from the premises. The reasoning process evolves from general to specific. In the case of an inductive reasoning the inference is based on facts. The hypotheses evolve from experience which becomes the basis for testing the hypotheses. The reasoning process evolves from specific to general. The diagnostic process is a classification process because the malfunctioning of the organism has to be categorized and labeled. The deductive component of the diagnostic process results in hypotheses which can be refuted by experience. The inductive component is based on sources as background knowledge and specific experience. The diagnostic process is a process of object identification by checking whether a symptom or combination of symptoms appears.

A diagnosis presupposes the availability of concepts. A concept is a rule for classifying objects in two (or more) subcategories representing exemplars of the concept (Hunt, 1962; Hovland, 1952). In order to acquire diagnostic skills conceptual knowledge is needed and can be provided through instruction, and this is the focus of this contribution. A model for the instruction for the learning of concepts is described by Merrill and Tennyson (1977) and Tennyson and Cocchiarella (1986). Merrill and Tennyson suppose that the learning of concepts consists of two phases. The first one is the formation of a prototype and the second is the acquisition of classificatory skills. From this assumption an instructional design model for the learning of concepts has been developed. This model has two basic components: content structure variables and instructional design variables. A rational combination of these components results in the selection of one of the four basic instructional design strategies. These strategies consist of manipulating the primary instructional design variables: a) definition, i.e. a rule or generality encompassing the structure of the critical attributes, b) expository instances, i.e. (non-)instances which organize the content in propositional format, c) interrogatory instances, i.e. (non-)instances which organize the content in interrogatory format, and d) attribute elaboration, i.e. analysis of critical attributes in expository instances and feedback as to critical attributes in interrogatory instances.

Although there is confirming evidence for the applicability of this model for learning concepts (Ok-Choon Park & Tennyson, 1980; Tennyson & Seong Ik Park, 1984) the effect of prototype formation on generalization to new instances and discrimination of instances from non-instances has hardly been investigated in the medical domain. In as far as it has been investigated (Cantor & Smith, 1980) it was found that physicians state that they are more confident about their diagnosis when the attributes of the disease are more representative. Though there is not much evidence for the applicability of the model in the medical domain, the model of Merrill and Tennyson (1977) and Tennyson and Cocchiarella (1986) seems promising for mainly two reasons. Firstly, the model is based on prototype theory (Posner & Keele, 1968; Rosch & Mervis, 1975). This approach is suitable for medical concepts because of the fact that medical concepts, especially diseases, vary in representativeness. The most representative or typical members share the most attributes with other members of a category. Secondly, the two basic components are generalization to new instances and discrimination of instances from non-instances. These components are central in the process of differential diagnosis of a disease.

The purpose of the experiment reported here is to test the hypothesis that decisions on class membership are facilitated if categorization takes place as a matching process between prototype and instance. Consistent with the assumptions of prototype theory it is expected that in the medical domain, as in other domains, a differential effect will be found as a result of prototype-based instruction.

METHOD

Subjects

A group of 106 subjects participated in the experiment. These subjects were recruited from a nurses' training college.

Material

An instructional program about the concept "shock" was developed. In this program the concept of shock is defined as a reduction of amount of blood in the organism. It is a state of circulatory insufficiency in which cellular perfusion is inadequate for normal cellular function. Shock is defined as a condition arising from hypovolemia, sepsis, cardiac disorders, anaphylactic reactions and neurogenic causes. Shock is a complex syndrome of cardiopulmonary, hemodynamic and vascular changes that reduce cellular perfusion and oxygen transport. The reduced cellular perfusion is caused by a loss of circulating fluid volume, pump failure or widespread vasodilation. In the instruction program five types of shock are differentiated. Hypovolemic shock is one of the most common types of shock. Profound hemorrhage is the usual precipitating factor of this type of shock, but it can also occur in patients who are severally dehydrated. Hypovolemic shock is a result of blood loss, loss of plasma or other body fluids. The symptoms are coolness of the skin, restlessness, hypotension, oliguria and increased rate and depth of respiration. Septic shock is caused by infection with a gram-negative bacterium but it may be associated with gram-positive infections. The patient may be cold and clammy with obviously poor peripheral perfusion, but can also present a warm and well circulated skin. Cardiogenic shock occurs when the heart is unable to pump enough blood to meet the body tissues need for oxygen. The most common precipitating factor of cardiogenic shock is myocardial infarction. The attributes of cardiogenic shock are absent or poor peripheral pulses, cold or clammy skin, systolic blood pressure less than 85mm Hg and urinary output less than 25 ml. Anaphylactic shock is the result of antigen-antibody reaction. The release of histamin, serotonin and bradykinin affects the blood vessels directly, causing vasodilation and increased capillary permeability. If the reduction in vasomotor tone occurs at the level of the vasomotor centre of the medulla the resulting generalized vasodilation is called neurogenic shock, i.e. a state in which neuro-control mechanics of peripheral vascular tone are interrupted. The general and specific attributes of the different types of shock are summarized in Table 1.

The instruction comprised three parts: 1) definition of shock; 2) causes and effects of shock; 3) types of shock. Part 1 consisted of three expository texts about the definition of shock. Each of these was followed by the presentation of a videotaped typical case of shock in the prototype condition, while in the attribute condition the attributes were listed sequentially. Part 2 comprised three expository texts about etiology and effects of shock. Part 3 consisted of two expository texts about hypovolemic shock, each of them followed by a videotaped typical case of hypovolemic shock in the prototype-based condition or by a listing of the attributes of hypovolemic shock. Secondly part 3 of the instruction contained expository texts about hypovolemic,

Table 1
Attributes of shock (general attributes in upper column, specific attributes in lowest columns)

	Shock	attributes: - paleness - coldness - perspiration - fast pulse rate - low blood pressure - reduced urinary output		
hypovolemic shock	cardiogenic shock	septic shock	anaphylactic shock	neurogenic shock
attributes:	attributes:	attributes:	attributes:	attributes:
- coolness of the skin - restlessness - hypotension - oliguria - increased rate of respiration	- poor periheral pulses - clammy skin - low systolic blood pressure - urinary output < 25ml/hr	- cold/clammy/ warm skin - poor peripheral perfusion - diminished urinary output - tachycardia - tachypnea	- irregular breathing - urticaria - erythema - vascular collapse	- irregular peripheral vascular tone - central nervous system failure

cardiogenic, neurogenic, septic and anaphylactic shock, all followed by videotaped typical cases of these types of shock or by enumeration of attributes.

Tests

During the instruction program two multiple-choice questions and two open-essay questions were presented to the students after each expository text. If their response was incorrect, feedback was provided and a second trial was given to respond correctly. The total number of items administered during instruction was 22. After the instruction an immediate posttest was administered. The first part of this test consisted of twelve questions, referring to the *definition of shock and the defining attributes* of types of shock: hypovolemic shock, cardiogenic shock, septical shock and anaphylactical shock (*definition*). The second part of the posttest consisted of five questions. In these questions attributes were provided and the students had to decide, whether they could infer to shock. If so, then they had to identify the *type of shock*. The scoring of the posttest was such that for the twelve questions referring to the definition of types of shock a maximum score of 5 points per item could be reached, while for the five questions referring to inference of a type of shock a maximum score of 10 points per item could be reached. The retention test consisted of ten composite cases of *shock or non-shock*. In each of the ten cases, students had to decide on shock or non-shock. This was the first component of the retention test. If they inferred to non-shock they had to identify the name of the observed disease. If they inferred to shock they had to list the five most salient attributes from a list (*inference*). This was the second component of the retention test. Students also had to identify the type of shock and to list the most salient differences and commonalities between pairs of cases of shock. This was the third component of the retention test (*classification*). The scoring of the retention test was such that for deciding on shock or non-shock two points could be acquired (maximum score: $10 \times 2 = 20$), for identifying the attributes one point per attribute could be acquired (maximum score: $10 \times 5 = 50$), and for identifying the types of shock in terms of differences and commonalities five points could be acquired for each comparison (maximum score: $5 \times 5 = 25$).The maximum total score was also $10 + 50 + 25 = 85$.

Procedure

The students (n= 104) were randomly divided in two groups (n_1= 49 and n_2= 55). They participated in a time-limited instructional program, which was implemented on TAIGA, an acronym for Twente Advanced Interactive Graphical Authoring system. The time limit was 1.5 hrs. Videotaped displays of typical cases of shock were provided separately on a video screen. The instructional program was provided by a computer network of Tulip-Compact.

The instructional procedures, according to which the information about shock was presented, can be described in terms of expository text, different types of questions and feedback. In the text-only condition (n= 49) as well as in the text+video condition (n= 55) the instruction began with an expository text about the generic concept of shock. This exposition was followed by 1 open-essay question and 1 multiple choice question. After feedback (where needed) a videotaped, typical case of shock was presented in the text+video condition. This information was mediated verbally in the text-only condition. This cycle of expository text about the generic aspects of shock, questioning and presentation (verbally or visually) of a typical case of shock was varied twice. This was the first part. The second part consisted of 3 expository texts about the causes of shock.Each exposition was followed by 1 open essay question and 1 multiple choice question. The third part module contained expository texts about 5 different types of shock (hypovolemic shock, cardiogenic shock, anaphylactic shock, neurogenic shock, septic shock). Each exposition was followed by questioning. In the text+video condition typical cases of hypovolemic shock, cardiogenic shock, neurogenic shock, anaphylactic shock and septic shock were presented visually. The information, contained in these typical cases, was presented verbally in the text-only condition.

RESULTS

Posttest: the mean score for the text-only condition for the first component (definition) of the posttest is 38.10 (SD= 8.88) and for the text+video condition 37.90 (SD= 9.37). This difference is not significant: t(102)=.11 (p= n.s.). The scores of this subtest are displayed in Figure 1.

The mean score for the text-only condition for the second component of the posttest (type identification) is 18.57 (SD= 7.30) and for the text+video condition 23.49 (SD= 7.58). This difference is significant: t(102)= -3.36 (p<0.01). The scores of this subtest are presented in Figure 2.

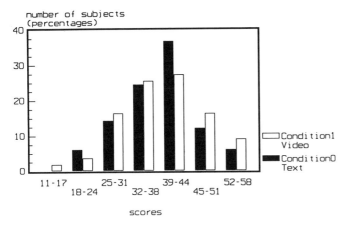

Figure 1. Comparison of scores of posttest 1: Definition.

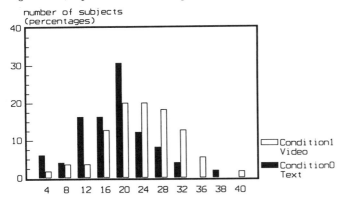

Figure 2. Comparison of scores of posttest 2: Type identification.

Retention test: the mean score for the text-only condition for the first component (shock/non-shock identification) of the retention test is 13.59 (SD= 2.24) and for the text+video condition 14.25 (SD=2.53). This difference is not significant: t(102)= - 1.41 (p< n.s.). The scores of this subtest are displayed in Figure 3.

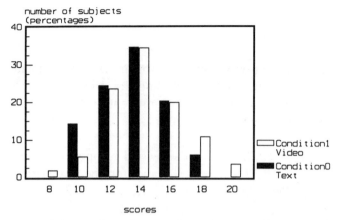

Figure 3. Comparison of scores of retention test 1: Shock/non-shock identification.

The mean score for the text-only condition for the second component (inference salient attributes) of the retention test is 25.41 (SD= 5.96) and for the text+video condition 27.07 (SD= 6.12). This difference is nog significant: t(102)= -1.41 (p< n.s.). The scores of this subtest are presented in Figure 4.

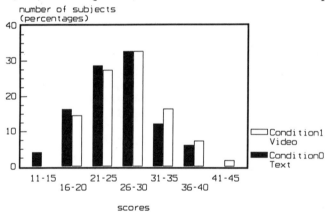

Figure 4. Comparison of scores of retention test 2: Inference salient attributes.

The mean score for the text-only condition for the third component (classification) of the retention test is 10.88 (SD= 2.03) and for the text+video condition 16.69 (SD= 2.21). This difference is significant: t(102)= -13.95 (p<0.01). The scores of this subtest are displayed in Figure 5.

The mean score for the text-only condition for the retention test as a whole is 50.18 (SD= 8.87) and for the text+video condition 58.20 (SD= 8.13). This difference is significant: t(102)= -4.81 (p<0.01). The scores for the retention test as a whole are presented in Figure 6.

Summarizing: Posttest 1 (definition), retention test 1 (shock/non-shock identification), and retention test 2 (inference salient attributes) do not yield

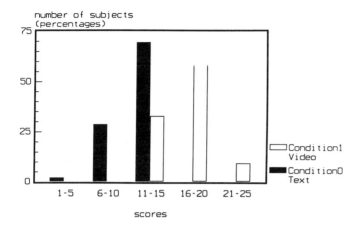

Figure 5. Comparison of scores of retention test 3: Classification.

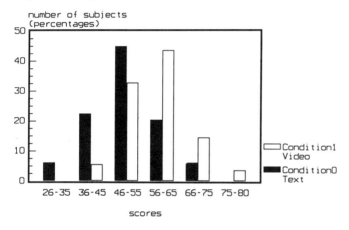

Figure 6. Comparison of scores of retention test 4: Overall.

significant differences. Posttest 2 (type identification), retention test 3 (classification) and retention test 4 (overall) do show significant differences between both conditions.

DISCUSSION

Classification of diseases can be explained through prototype theory (Rosch, 1978; Merrill & Tennyson, 1977). Prototype theory is focussed on processes of acquisition, organization and representation of information in terms of prototypes, regarded as typical cases of a category. In this experiment a prototype-based instruction has been investigated as to its differential effects on the categorization of non-encountered types of shock. It was expected that, when typical cases of shock encompassing defining as well as irrelevant attributes were presented in the prototype condition, this would result in an increase of the ability to discriminate between different types of shock and of the ability to generalize to new instances of shock. Analysis of the data provides confirming evidence for this hypothesis.

One has to realize that complex entities like shock can only be defined unequivocally in terms of similarity to the most typical case of the concept. This point of view is consistent with the hypothesis of Rosch (1975) that an item is more or less a representative member of a category. She assumes that categories resemble correlates in reality. Evidence for this correlation is the fact that certain categories co-occur very frequently. As to the structure of the attributes Rosch exemplifies her view by stating that the relations between entities are expressed on different levels. A superordinate level is characterized by a higher degree of abstraction. The potential number of subordinate entities on a higher level is greater than the potential number of a lower level. Within the hierarchy there is a necessary implication as to the numbers of elements which are part of a certain level. There is an asymmetrical relation between levels as exemplified by the proposition that a poodle is a dog, but a dog is not necessarily a poodle (subordinate level). Within the prototype paradigm there are also three levels: subordinate level, basic level and superordinate level. For human beings it is easier to make a visual representation of entities on a level which is clearly connected to certain objects. This level has been identified by Rosch as the basic level (Rosch, 1978; 1975). Categories on this level are learned first. For human beings it is much easier to construct sentences with basic categories than with other types of categories. When perceiving the environment, basic categories are recognized primarily (Rosch, 1978; Fodor, 1983). Basic categories have a lower degree of abstractness compared with members on a higher or lower level. Basic categories tend to coincide with information peaks. Rosch showed that students who professed to make an image or representation on the superordinate level did this by an image of one or more instances on the basic level. The basic level seems the most inclusive level at which the correlational structure of the world comes into existence. In forming a prototype the basic level of concepts plays a crucial role, as has been confirmed in this experiment. Presenting a prototype of shock does result in a mental image of the shock patient which is more resistant to extinction than propositional information about the shock patient. This result has to be interpreted in terms of the fact that at the basic level of concept representation a prototype encompasses both the most frequent occurring attributes as well as irrelevant attributes. As such the result of this experiment forms a corroboration of the model as proposed by Rosch and of the tranfer of this model to the context of an instructional design guide for learning concepts as proposed by Merrill and Tennyson. The learning of complex medical concepts like shock can be facilitated to the degree that defining and irrelevant attributes of the concept to be learned are presented at the basic level.

REFERENCES

Bruner, J.S., Goodnow, J.J., & Austin G.A. (1956). *A study of thinking.* New York: Wiley.

Cantor, N., & Smith, E.E. (1980). Psychiatric diagnosis as prototype categorisation. *Journal of Abnormal Psychology, 89* (2), 181-193.

Elstein, A.S., Shulman, L.S., & Sprafka, S. (1978). *Medical problem solving.* Cambridge: Harvard University Press.

Fodor, J.A. (1983). *The modularity of mind.* Cambridge: M.I.T. Press.

Hunt, E.B. (1962). *Concept learning: an information processing problem.* New York: Wiley.

Hovland, C.I.A. (1952). A communication analysis of concept learning. *Psychological Review, 59,* 461-472.

Merrill, M.D., & Tennyson, R.D. (1977). *Teaching concepts: An instructional design guide.* Englewood Cliffs, NJ: Educational Technology Publications.

Ok-Choon Park, & Tennyson, R.D. (1980). Adaptive design strategies for selecting number and presentation order of examples in coordinate concept acquisition. *Journal of Educational Psychology, 72*(3), 362-370.

Posner, M.I., & Keele, S.W. (1968). On the genesis of abstract ideas. *Journal of Experimental Psychology, 77,* 353-363.

Rosch, E. (1975). Cognitive representations of semantic categories. *Journal of Experimental Psychology: General, 104,* 192-233.

Rosch, E. (1978). Principles of categorizations. In E. Rosch & B.B. Lloyd (Eds.), *Cognition and categorization* (pp. 24-46). Hillsdale, NJ: Lawrence Erlbaum Associates.

Rosch, E., & Mervis, C.B. (1975). Family resemblances: Studies in the internal structure of categories. *Cognitive Psychology, 7,* 573-605.

Tennyson, R.D., & Park, S.I. (1984). Process learning time as an adaptive design variable in concept learning using computer-based instruction. *Journal of Educational Psychology, 76,* 452-465.

Tennyson, R.D., & Cocchiarella, M. (1986). An empirically based instructional design theory for teaching concepts. *Review of Educational Research, 56*(1), 40-71.

9

INSTRUCTIONAL DESIGN FOR TEACHING CONCEPTS: DO THE NUMBER AND DISPERSION OF EXAMPLES INFLUENCE THE ABSTRACTION OF A COGNITIVE MODEL OF A CONCEPT?

Hendrik H. Leemkuil
University of Twente

ABSTRACT

Students learning a new concept will try to structure the new information in order to form a cognitive model of the concept. Research indicates that the cognitive model of a concept is not just a summary of those features that are necessary and (jointly) sufficient to define the concept, but that it also contains information about variable and irrelevant features of the concept. Rosch (1978) pointed out that a cognitive model is not a cluster of independent features related by some kind of rule, but a correlational structure, a contextual entity. In this article research is reported concerning two variables which are presumed to influence the abstraction of a cognitive model. The two variables are: the number of visually presented examples and the dispersion of the examples. It was hypothesized that the abstraction of a cognitive model is facilitated when the number of examples increases and furthermore that a broad dispersion of examples enhances the ability to generalize the concept, while a narrow dispersion of examples facilitates the abstraction of a prototype.

INTRODUCTION

In their instructional design guide for teaching concepts, Merrill and Tennyson (1977) state that the structural form of the information presented to the student clearly affects the form of the knowledge coded in memory. The research reported in this article concerns two variables which are presumed to influence the cognitive model a student tries to form of a concept. Before giving a detailed description of the research, first a short overview of the theoretical background will be given.

How is knowledge about a given concept stored in memory? In certain theories about concept learning (see Smith & Medin, 1981 and De Klerk, 1987) it is assumed that the representation of a concept is a summary description of an entire class. The features included in the description are all singly necessary and jointly sufficient to define that concept. For a feature to be singly necessary, every instance of the concept *must* have it; for a set of features to be jointly sufficient, every entity having that set must be an instance of the concept. Research (Hampton, 1979, and Rosch & Mervis, 1975) indicated that the cognitive representation is not a mere reflection of the definition of a concept, but entails more. People use nonnecessary features in categorization. This implies that those features are also part of the cognitive representation.

Rosch (1978) suggests that concepts are coded in memory neither as lists or sets of hypotheses of defining criteria (critical attributes) necessary for determining class inclusion, nor as lists of individual instances (class members). Rather, concepts are coded in memory as contextual entities, i.e. correlational structures of meaningful dimensions. Tennyson and Cocchiarella (1986) agree with her and so does Lakoff (1987). He states that concepts are represented in memory as cognitive models (roughly equivalent to Rumelhart's "schemas" and Schank & Abelson's "scripts"). Some concepts/categories are characterized by clusters of cognitive models. "Mother" is a concept that is based on a complex model in which a number of individual cognitive models converge, forming an experiential cluster:
-   The birth model: the person giving birth is the mother.
-   The genetic model: the female who contributed the genetic material is the mother.
-   The nurturance model: the female adult who nurtures and raises a child is the mother of the child.
-   The marital model: the wife of the father is the mother.
-   The genealogical model: the closest female ancestor is the mother.

When the cluster of models that jointly characterize a concept diverge there is still a strong pull to view one as the most important. Lakoff further points out that cognitive models are *idealized*. Sometimes they refer to abstract ideal cases.

The internal structure of a cognitive model or a cluster of models plays an important role in categorization. It accounts for certain effects which Rosch and her co-workers have shown to exist. They found, for example, that subjects needed more time to classify a penguin or chicken as a bird than for instance a robin or a sparrow. This phenomenon can be explained by the idealized nature of cognitive models. When a particular example looks very much like the average category member it tends to be classified faster. Rosch calls this a prototype effect. Prototypes are described by Rosch (1978) as those members of a category that most reflect the redundancy structure of the category as a whole.

She stresses that prototypes do not constitute a theory of representation of categories. Prototype abstraction, however, plays an important role in learning concepts. It constrains the cognitive representation of a concept students try to form.

Several studies have examined differences in prototype abstraction as a function of type of training. The variables studied were number of examples and their dispersion from the prototype. As summarized by Wickelgren (1979), the results of the experiments showed that an increase in the number of examples caused an increase in prototype abstraction and the ability to classify new examples. A narrow dispersion of examples facilitated prototype abstraction, because in this case all the examples strongly resembled each other and the prototype. The generalization of the concept to more broadly dispersed examples required more training examples to cover the desired larger region of the attribute space adequately.

The materials used in the experiments generally consisted of artificially constructed objects like dot-patterns (Posner & Keele, 1968; Homa & Vosburgh, 1976; Breen & Schvaneveldt, 1986; Busemeyer & Myung, 1988), of which the number of irrelevant features is usually small. The hypotheses about type of training should also be tested with ecologically valid school subject matter. Only a few experiments using school subject matter have been reported. Tennyson, Youngers and Suebsonthi (1983) used the concept "regular polygon". But this is still a concept with only a few variable features (size and colour). Gerritsen van der Hoop (1984) used a more complicated concept: "social control".

In the experiment to be reported (cf. Ranzijn, 1987) a concept from biology will be used. Two variables will be manipulated independently: the dispersion of the examples and the number of examples, as shown on a videotape.

It is hypothesized that presenting more visual examples will enhance prototype abstraction and therefore will enable the students to form a better cognitive model of the concept. It is further hypothesized that subjects presented with the broadly dispersed examples will increase their ability to classify progressively more items correctly, compared to those who get the narrowly dispersed examples, because they have a more valid representation of the breadth of the category. Finally it is predicted that subjects presented with the narrowly dispersed examples will be more accurate in producing a verbal description of the concept, because the variable features of the examples presented have a high degree of similarity. Therefore, these subjects are more easily focused on the critical features.

METHOD

Subjects

40 Sixth-grade elementary school pupils between the age of 11 and 12 participated in the experiment. Four matched groups were formed on the basis of general school ability (judged by the teachers) of the students.

Design

A 2 x 2 experimental design was used to test the hypotheses. The first independent variable, dispersion of the examples, consisted of two levels: narrow or broad dispersion. Narrow dispersion means that the examples are centered round the prototype. The examples have variable features which occur frequently. Broad dispersion means that the examples differ from the prototype and that they have variable features which occur less frequently. The second independent variable, the number of visually presented examples, likewise consisted of two levels: one or four videorecordings were given in addition to the written descriptions of examples (more about the differences between the four experimental treatments in the next paragraph). Test scores were the dependent variables.

Program

An instructional computer program describing the concept windflower was designed. Windflowers are a category of flowers of which the pollen is transferred from one flower to the other by the wind (in another category of flowers this is done by animals). The program consisted of three parts: the elements of a flower, the principle of pollination and a description of windflowers. The last part consisted of six episodes. The first two described windflowers in general, the other four described four particular windflowers.

The differences between the four treatment conditions became manifest in the last episodes of the instructional program. Three of the four examples in the narrow-examples conditions differed from the broad-examples conditions (see Table 1). Subjects in the one-example conditions were presented the same (four) written descriptions of flowers but saw a video of only one flower (the first one).

Apparatus

The computer program was presented on an Apple Macintosh Plus (1Mb) microcomputer. Attached to the microcomputer was a Panasonic AG-6200 videorecorder, using a BCD-controller as interface. The videorecordings were presented on a Philips CM8833 colour monitor.

Table 1
The experimental treatments

	Written descriptions of:	1	4
Narrow	- cock's foot	video	video
	- stinging nettle	-	video
	- hazel	-	video
	- reed	-	video
Broad	- hazel	video	video
	- dock	-	video
	- needle-leaved tree	-	video
	- grass	-	video

Tests

Two kinds of test were given: a classification test and a test of declarative knowledge.

The first test was the classification test. The students were given a pile of 35 pictures of flowers and were asked to pick out the windflowers (n = 17).

Colour is a very salient feature of flowers. Flowers which are pollinated by animals usually have very salient colours (red, yellow etc.) to attract the animals. Windflowers usually don't have a salient colour because they do not have to attract animals (most of them are greenish or brownish). So by looking at only the colour of the flower you have a chance of more than 50% to correctly classify a flower as a windflower. To determine whether or not students could also classify flowers without the colour cue, black and white pictures were included in the test.

It is assumed that some flowers can be more easily classified when the photograph is in colour and others when the photograph is in black & white. Because this could influence the data, two different versions of the test were used. Test A consisted of 18 colour (9 windflowers) and 17 black and white photographs (8 windflowers). Test B consisted of 17 colour (8 windflowers) and 18 black and white photographs (9 windflowers). A black and white picture in test A is in colour in test B. The number of correctly classified flowers (windflower or not a windflower) was scored.

The second test consisted of two questions: 1) Imagine that you had to tell a friend what a windflower looks like. How would you do that? Write a short story of what you would say. 2) Mention some examples of windflowers. The number of correct features mentioned in the story and the number of correct examples were scored.

Procedure

The subjects were first shown a computer program that explained how to work with the computer, which required about 5 to 6 minutes. Then the instructional program was presented requiring 20 to 25 minutes. The tests were administered after the subjects had played a computer game for 5 minutes. Subjects were first administered the classification test. Half of the students in one treatment condition got test A, the other half test B.

RESULTS

The mean test scores are presented in Table 2.

Table 2
Mean test scores as a function of number of examples and the dispersion of examples

Condition	Classification		Features		Examples	
	Mean	(SD)	M	(SD)	M	(SD)
Narrow 1	21.20	(4.08)	1.00	(1.88)	1.50	(0.97)
Narrow 4	20.60	(3.69)	0.70	(1.33)	1.60	(0.84)
Broad 1	22.70	(5.87)	0.20	(0.63)	0.50	(0.97)
Broad 4	24.90	(3.38)	0.80	(0.63)	1.00	(1.25)

A multivariate analysis of variance on the test scores revealed a significant effect of the dispersion of the examples, $F(3,36)=6.60$, $p=0.001$. The results of the analysis are shown in Table 3.

Table 3
Results of the analysis of variance of the dispersion and the number of examples (and their interaction) on the post test scores

	Multivariate				Univariate		
Source	F	df	p	Dep.var.	F	df	p
Disp.	6.60	3,36	0.001	Class.	4.49	1,38	0.041
				Features	0.81	1,38	0.374
				Examples	6.28	1,38	0.017
Number	0.28	3,36	0.837	Class.	0.31	1,38	0.582
				Features	0.15	1,38	0.704
				Examples	0.77	1,38	0.385
Inter.	0.61	3,36	0.614	Class.	1.03	1,38	0.317
				Features	1.32	1,38	0.258
				Examples	0.39	1,38	0.539

Classification ability

Univariate analysis of variance on the classification test scores yielded a significant effect for dispersion: the subjects of the broad example groups made more correct classifications, F(1,38)= 4.49, p= 0.041 (see Figure 1).

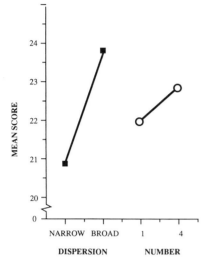

Figure 1. Mean scores on the classification test for each of the two groups on each independent variable.

Declarative knowledge

ANOVA of the mean number of correct features mentioned showed no significant effects. ANOVA of the mean number of correct examples mentioned yielded a significant effect for dipersion: the subjects of the narrow example groups mentioned significantly more correct examples of the windflower category, F(1,38)= 6.28, p= 0.017 (see Figure 2).

Difference between colour and black & white pictures

If the mean number of correctly classified photographs is split up into colour and black & white pictures it appears that almost as many colour photographs (51.2%) as black & white photographs (48.8%) are classified correctly (see Table 4).

DISCUSSION

The first independent variable, dispersion of examples, has a significant impact on the data. As expected the subjects in the broad dispersion groups classified more photographs correctly than those in the narrow dispersion groups (see Figure 1). The narrow dispersion groups however performed

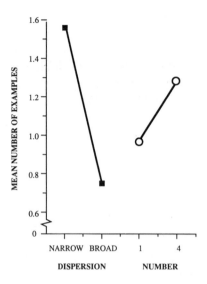

Figure 2. Mean number of correct examples mentioned for each of the two groups on each independent variable.

Table 4
Mean number of correctly classified photograhps split into colour and black & white photographs

Condition	Colour	Black & White
Narrow 1	11.2 (52.8%)	10.0 (47.2%)
Narrow 4	10.4 (50.5%)	10.2 (49.5%)
Broad 1	11.3 (49.8%)	11.4 (50.2%)
Broad 4	12.9 (51.8%)	12.0 (48.2%)

better on the test of declarative knowledge, especially on the second question (see Figure 2). It can be assumed that the subjects in these groups pay more attention to the critical features and the verbal description of the flower because the examples are very much alike, whereas in the broad dispersion groups subjects pay more attention to the variable features.

These results are in line with what was expected, but are in contrast with what Gerritsen van der Hoop (1984) found. He found that giving varied examples enhances performance when people have to generate new examples (of the concept "social control") but not if they have to classify situation descriptions.

The results further indicate that the number of visually presented examples does not influence the data significantly. Especially between the narrow dispersion groups there are no big differences. Between the broad dispersion groups the differences are bigger and are always in favour of the group which saw four examples (see Figures 1 and 2). So subjects profit more from seeing more examples when the examples differ considerably from each other. This could have been expected.

The effect of the number of visually presented examples may have been reduced by the fact that the students already knew a lot of the flowers which were given as examples. For example, almost everybody knows what a stinging nettle looks like. Although one doesn't know that it is a (wind)flower, one already has a mental image of it. So, when a subject reads that a stinging nettle is an example of the category of windflowers, the mental image of the flower is activated. If the mental image is accurate then it is not necessary to see a video recording of it.

The data in Table 4 show that the subjects on the whole didn't classify more colour pictures correct than black & white pictures. So the subjects on the whole were able to classify pictures of flowers when the colour cue was not present as well as when it was present. As expected there are some exceptions. For instance the Juncacea effusus (a windflower) was classified correctly by 12 pupils when the photograph was in black & white and by 7 pupils when it was in colour, and the Polygonacea persicaria (peach wort, not a windflower) was classified correctly by 6 pupils when the photograph was in black & white and by 18 pupils when it was in colour.

All in all, the results are in line with the expectations and the findings of experiments carried out with artificial concepts (see Wickelgren, 1979). What are the implications for the instructional design for teaching concepts? Tennyson and Cocchiarella (1986) view concept learning as a two phase-process: a) formation of conceptual knowledge and b) development of procedural knowledge. On the basis of the experimental data one can say that in the first phase it is best to give some examples that closely resemble each other (centered around the prototype). In the second phase it is best to give examples that are broadly dispersed. Giving more examples in this phase will lead to a better cognitive model of the concept and will enable the student to generalize the concept more broadly.

REFERENCES

Breen, T.J., & Schvaneveldt, R.W. (1986). Classification of empirically derived prototypes as a function of category experience. *Memory & Cognition, 14*(4), 313-320.

Busemeyer, J.R., & Myung, I.J. (1988). A new method for investigating prototype learning. *Journal of Experimental Psychology: Learning, Memory, and Cognition, 14*(1), 3-11.

De Klerk, L.F.W. (1987). The teaching and learning of concepts. In P.R.J. Simons & G. Beukhof (Eds.), *Regulation of learning* (pp. 137-148). Den Haag: SVO.

Gerritsen van der Hoop, J.W. (1984). De rol van gevarieerde voorbeelden bij het leren van begrippen [The effect of varied examples in learning concepts]. In L.F.W. De Klerk & A.M.P. Knoers (Eds.), *Onderwijs-psychologisch onderzoek* (Educational psychological research) (pp. 154-163). Lisse: Swets & Zeitlinger.

Hampton, J.A. (1979). Polymorphous concepts in semantic memory. *Journal of Verbal Learning and Verbal Behavior, 18*, 441-461.

Homa, D., & Vosburgh, R. (1976). Category breadth and the abstraction of prototypical information. *Journal of Experimental Psychology: Human Learning and memory, 2*, 322-330.

Lakoff, G. (1987). Cognitive models and prototype theory. In U. Neisser (Ed.), *Concepts and conceptual development* (pp. 63-100). Cambridge: Cambridge University Press.

Merrill, M.D., & Tennyson, R.D. (1977). *Teaching concepts: An instructional design guide.* Englewood Cliffs, NJ: Educational technology Publications.

Posner, M.I., & Keele, S.W. (1968). On the genesis of abstract ideas. *Journal of Experimental Psychology, 77*, 353-363.

Ranzijn, F.J.A. (1987). The example presentation form and concept learning. In P.R.J. Simons & G. Beukhof (Eds.), *Regulation of learning* (pp. 167-174). Den Haag: SVO.

Rosch, E. (1978). Principles of categorization. In E. Rosch & B.B. Lloyd (Eds.), *Cognition and categorization* (pp. 27-48). Hillsdale, NJ: Lawrence Erlbaum.

Rosch, E., & Mervis, C.B. (1975). Family resemblance studies in the internal structure of categories. *Cognitive Psychology, 3*, 382-439.

Smith, E.E., & Medin, D.L. (1981). *Categories and concepts.* Cambridge: Harvard University Press.

Tennyson, R.D., & Cocchiarella, M.J. (1986). An empirically based instructional design theory for teaching concepts. *Review of Educational Research, 56*(1), 40-71.

Tennyson, R.D., Youngers, J., & Suebsonthi, P. (1983). Concept learning by children using instructional presentation forms for prototype formation and classification-skill development. *Journal of Educational Psychology, 75*(2), 280-291.

Wickelgren, W.A. (1979). *Cognitive psychology.* Englewood Cliffs: Prentice-Hall.

10

THE EXAMPLE PRESENTATION FORM IN INSTRUCTION FOR NATURAL CONCEPTS

Frederik J.A. Ranzijn
University of Twente

ABSTRACT

In the study reported here, an instructional design based on the prototype view is presented. The effects of two forms of example presentation on concept learning were investigated. In one condition, examples were presented as line drawings on a microcomputer monitor, in the other condition the example was presented "real life" on a video monitor. The hypothesis that the realistic presentation would lead to a better classification skill could be confirmed. It is assumed that the subject's familiarity with the material (preconceptions) has influenced the results.[1]

INTRODUCTION

In the classical view of concept learning all instances of a concept share common properties and these are separately necessary and jointly sufficient (Smith & Medin, 1981). Those properties of the objects used in a classification rule are the defining or relevant properties, the others are the variable or irrelevant properties. Experiments designed to study concept learning from the classical point of view mostly used well defined, artificial concepts. The set of objects to be classified almost always consisted of a finite number of objects, particularly geometrical figures, and were used to study the external conditions of concept learning, i.e. the characteristics of the set of objects and the relations between the characteristics.

The classical view was criticized by the prototype view (Posner and Keele, 1968; Neumann, 1974, 1977; Rosch and Mervis, 1975; Rosch, 1978) which is focusing more on natural categories with fuzzy boundaries. According to the prototype view not all members of a category are equally representative and the properties are not necessarily shared by all members, rather members vary in the degree in which they are judged to be good examples of the category. The classical view does not deal with the internal representation of concepts and is not able to explain for instance that the reaction time to determine category membership is longer for some objects than for others belonging to the same category (Rosch, 1976). Another criticism of the classical studies of concept attainment is that they lack representativeness of the "real life processes", by the use of "artificial" concepts.

Most research on concept learning is done by teaching subjects a new concept or concepts and by studying the learning process. The rules for instructional design for concept learning closely follow the classical view, i.e. are mainly fixed to the defining attributes. Klausmeier and his collaborators (Klausmeier, Ghatala & Frayer,1974; Klausmeier & Sipple, 1980) presented a cognitive theory of learning and development. In their instructional design rules, they focus mainly on the concept definition and the defining attributes. According to the instructional design guide of Merrill and Tennyson (1977), the most effective way to teach a concept is to present a definition, followed by several examples and some practice.

In his later work Tennyson made a shift towards the application of the prototype theory (Tennyson, Chao, & Youngers, 1981; Tennyson, Youngers & Suebsonthi, 1983). Tennyson et al. (1983) presented a model of concept-learning that includes two learning processes: formation in the memory of information representative of a given concept class, and the development of the cognitive skills of generalization and discrimination. They concluded that "in an initial exposure to a concept, a best example may facilitate encoding of a clear prototype from which learners can both add specific dimensions and begin classification-skill development". In addition they concluded that presentation of a best example is preferable to presenting an operational rule that offers the relations between the concept definition and the critical attributes. The learner is encoding an abstraction of the concept class as a prototype and the dimensionality of the prototype in relation to the variable descriptors is elaborated by presenting succeeding examples. In this study the concept "regular polygon" was taught. This concept has only two variable attributes (size and the number of angles).

Most natural categories (animals, plants, etc.) have more than one or two variable attributes. Most objects from natural categories can be classified in more than one category. A robin can be classified as a bird but also as a vertebrate. This makes it not clear what the best example is, and so picking out a best example is thus not always possible. In teaching natural categories the teacher has to present more than one example.

The presentation of examples can be done by presenting the real object, a realistic representation of the object (photograph or film), or by presenting a schematic representation (a line drawing). Presenting the real object can be difficult or impossible if the object is very large or not available. With the presentation of a photograph of a static object, or a film of a moving object or process, the variable attributes are still available and is it possible to form a prototype. In a schematic representation of the object the variable attributes are not available and prototype formation is impaired or impossible.

Concept learning can be viewed as a two-phase process: (a) the formation of conceptual knowledge, i.e. the integrated storage of meaningful dimensions selected from known examples, and (b) development of procedural knowledge by using conceptual knowledge to use domain-specific problems (Tennyson & Cocchiarella, 1986).

In this study it was tested whether the formation of a prototype is facilitated by the presentation form of the examples. In relation to the findings of Tennyson et al. (1983), it was hypothesized that if subjects are able to pay attention both to the defining attributes and to the variable attributes of the concept in a realistic presentation on video, prototype formation is facilitated, and would be better than when subjects do not have this opportunity in a schematic presentation. Consequently, on a categorization test these subjects would perform better.

The expected beneficial effect in the video condition will not be noticed on an immediate post test, and because of the "freshness" of the new information, both groups will perform equally well. After some time a decay of declarative knowledge will be noticed in both groups. However, for the procedural knowledge we expect that subjects in the video condition will perform better on a retention test than subjects in the other condition, because of a better consolidated prototype.

METHOD

Subjects

Twenty-nine subjects participated in this study. They were male and female pupils of a Dutch secondary school, aged between 12 and 15 years. The subjects were randomly chosen from the first grade group. Participation in this study was obligatory. The scores on the tests, however, were not included in their school grades. The pupils were randomly assigned to the conditions.

Design

In a repeated measurements design the hypothesis was tested. The independent variable, the example presentation form, consisted of three conditions: a video condition, in which the examples in the instructional program were realistically presented on a video monitor, a line drawing condition in which the same instances as in the first condition were presented as line drawings on a microcomputer screen, and a control condition in which we wanted to control the effects of presence of all the equipment in the video condition. In the program section we will elaborate on the control condition.

Program

An instructional computer program describing pollination was designed using the PETRIL authoring system (Sikken, 1987). The concepts to be learned were: wind-flowers (flowers of which the pollen is transported by the wind) and insect-flowers (flowers of which the pollen is transported by insects). The program consisted of the following parts: the elements of the flower, pollination, the concept of a wind-flower, the concept of an insect-flower, a synthesis (in which a summary was given of both concepts), and a small test in which some declarative knowledge was tested. The subject matter had not yet been taught in school.

The instructional parts consisted of successively presented windows with text. In some cases the window also contained a line drawing. In each window was a question about the content of that window. The next window was presented only if the question was answered correctly. The parts concerning wind-flowers and insect-flowers started with a window about the particular concept in general. Next the defining characteristics were explained, one at a time. After answering the question, an example was presented. The examples all had a duration of 20 seconds. The text in the line drawing fragments was spoken in the video fragments. It took the subjects about thirty to forty minutes to study the twenty windows of the program.

In the control condition the examples were the same instances as in the video condition, but we did not "zoom in", and thus did not offer the subjects enough detailed visual information to form a prototype.

Tests

Test of procedural knowledge
A classification test consisted of 8 photographs of wind-flowers and 7 photographs of insect-flowers. Insect-flowers mostly have very salient colours (yellow, red, etc.), and wind-flowers are almost always greenish or brownish. Just paying attention to the colour characteristic could possibly result in a high score. By also presenting pictures in black and white, we wanted study the effect of the colour cue.

Test of declarative knowledge
In this test the subjects were asked to recall the characteristics of the wind-flowers and the insect-flowers and give some examples of both.

Apparatus

The instructional program ran on an Apple Macintosh Plus (1Mb) microcomputer, connected with a Panasonic AG-6200 videorecorder, using a BCD-controller as interface. The video pictures were presented on a Philips CM8833 colour-monitor.

Procedure

Each subject individually studied the instructional computer program. The experimenter was positioned in such way that he could follow the progress and read the answers the subject gave to the questions asked by the program. If the subject did not manage to answer a question in the instruction part correctly in three trials, the correct answer was provided. After the instruction the classification test was given. After the classification test, the declarative knowledge test was given. After a two month interval both the procedural knowledge test (classification test) and the declarative knowledge test (retention tests) were taken again.

Data

Procedural knowledge data
The following scores were collected with the classification test: the number of correctly classified colour pictures of wind-flowers (COL.WIND), black and white pictures of wind-flowers (BLW.WIND), colour pictures of insect-flowers (COL.INS), black and white pictures of insect-flowers (BLW.INS). The total correct classifications of wind-flowers were calculated (WIND.TOT), the total correct insect-flowers (INS.TOT), and the total correct classifications (TOTAL).

Declarative knowledge data
The declarative knowledge test resulted in six scores: the number of defining characteristics correctly mentioned of each concept (CHAR.WIND, CHAR.INS), the number of examples given that were also in the program, i.e. recalled examples (WIND.REC, INS.REC), and the number of new or generated examples (WIND.GEN, INS.GEN).

RESULTS

Procedural knowledge

A univariate analysis of variance (ANOVA) on the classification test scores revealed no significant effect on the immediate post test. On the retention test significant effects are found on the variables WIND.TOT ($F = 2.80, p < .07$)

and TOTAL ($F = 5.08$, $p < .01$)(see Table 1). Two months after the instruction, subjects in the video condition classified the pictures best, followed by the subjects in the line drawing condition. The subjects in the control condition performed worst.

Table 1
ANOVA Results

	Post test			Retention Test		
variable	df.	F	p <	df.	F	p <
COL.WIND	2,23	2.72	.08	2,26	1.76	.19
BLW.WIND	2,23	.18	.83	2,26	.85	.43
COL.INS	2,23	3.34	.05	2,26	.30	.74
BLW.INS	2,23	.12	.88	2,26	.99	.38
WIND.TOT	2,23	1.76	.19	2,26	2.80	.07
INS.TOT	2,23	1.29	.29	2,26	1.27	.29
TOTAL	2,23	.02	.97	2,26	5.08	.01

Declarative knowledge

Univariate analysis of variance revealed no significant effect of the example presentation form on the scores of the declarative knowledge test, nor on the immediate post test nor on the retention test.

Difference scores

While procedural knowledge is generally increasing over time, declarative knowledge remains the same or is decreasing, although these differences (increase and decrease) are not significant.

DISCUSSION

We find an indication that subjects use a prototype on the retention test in the fact that the procedural knowledge is increasing while the declarative knowledge is not, and in the fact that the subjects in the control condition performed worst. Starting out from the classical point of view the classification test would be executed on basis of necessary and jointly sufficient properties (in other words, on basis of declarative knowledge). However, the procedural knowledge is increasing while the declarative knowledge is not. The classical point of view is unable to solve these "contrasting" results since an increase in classification score can only be achieved if an increase in declarative knowledge is also measured. Prototype theory can deal with this "classical" dilemma. The difference in procedural knowledge scores can be explained by a better consolidated prototype for subjects in the video condition. We were able to confirm our hypothesis that the presentation of visually richer examples would lead to a richer or better consolidated prototype.

On the retention test no effect was found for the scores on the variable INS.TOT, the total number of correctly classified insect-flowers. This could be the case for the following reason. It is quite likely that the subjects already had a prototype of a "flower" at hand. This prototype will probably be an insect-flower (great corolla, salient colours). What actually might have happened in the instruction is that the subjects learned that the "non-flower-like" flowers can be called "wind-flowers" and that the "flower-like" flowers can be called "insect-flowers". So, in fact only one new concept was taught: the concept of a "wind-flower" and the concept of a "flower" got a new label: "insect-flower". This would explain why an effect of the example presentation form was found only for the WIND.TOT and TOTAL variables.

So in classifying our test items the following rule would also lead to a high score: the more typical "flower" the test item is, the greater the possibility that it is an "insect-flower". The subject's familiarity with the material might strongly have influenced the results. In other words: we do not exactly know what procedural knowledge our subjects were using, or, stated differently, on what prototype(s) their classifications were based. In a new study we should use less familiar material and ask our subjects not only to classify objects but also ask for the procedure they use.

In this study it is demonstrated that subjects do not classify on basis of their declarative knowledge but that they use a prototype, and that the more realistic the encountered examples are, the better the prototype is.

Note

1.   This study was supported by a grant of the Institute for Educational Research (S.V.O.), grant no. 6620. The author wishes to thank S. Dijkstra, H.H. Leemkuil and D. Poppe for their support during this study and the management and students of Scholen-gemeenschap Zuid, Enschede, The Netherlands, for their friendly co-operation.

REFERENCES

Klausmeier, H.J., Ghatala, E.S., & Frayer, D. A. (1974). *Conceptual learning and development: A cognitive view.* New York: Academic Press.

Klausmeier, H.J., & Sipple, T.S. (1980). *Learning and teaching concepts: A strategy for testing applications of a theory.* New York: Academic Press.

Merrill, M.D., & Tennyson, R.D. (1977). *Teaching concepts: An instructional design guide.* Englewood Cliffs, NJ: Educational Technology Publications.

Neumann, P.G. (1974). An attribute frequency model for the abstraction of prototypes. *Memory and Cognition, 2,* 241-248.

Neumann, P.G. (1977). Visual prototype formation with discontinuous representation of dimensions of variability. *Memory and Cognition, 5*(2), 187-197.

Posner, M.I., & Keele, S.W. (1968). On the genesis of abstract ideas. *Journal of Experimental Psychology, 77,* 353-363.

Rosch, E. (1978). Principles of categorization. In E. Rosch & B.B. Lloyd (Eds.), *Cognition and categorization* (pp. 27-48). Hillsdale, NJ: Erlbaum.

Rosch, E., & Mervis, C.B. (1975). Family resemblances: Studies in the internal structure of categories. *Cognitive Psychology, 7,* 573-605.

Rosch, E., Simpson, C., & Miller, R.S. (1976). Structural bases of typicality effects. *Journal of Experimental Psychology: Human Perception and Performance, 9,* 491-502.

Sikken, J. (1987). *MPW Petril Manual* [Computer program manual]. Enschede, The Netherlands: University of Twente, Department of Education.

Smith, E.E., & Medin, D.L. (1981). *Categories and concepts.* Cambridge: Harvard University Press.

Tennyson, R.D., Chao, J.N., & Youngers, J. (1981). Concept learning effectiveness using prototype and skill development presentation forms. *Journal of Educational Psychology, 73,* 326-334.

Tennyson, R.D., & Cocchiarella, M.J. (1986). An empirically based instructional design theory for teaching concepts. *Review of Educational Research, 56*(1), 40-71.

Tennyson, R.D., Youngers, J., & Suebsonthi, P. (1983). Concept learning by children using instructional presentation forms for prototype formation and classification-skill development. *Journal of Educational Psychology, 75*(2), 280-291.

11

THE DESIGN OF ADAPTIVE INSTRUCTIONAL SYSTEMS FOR CONCEPT-LEARNING USING DECISION THEORY

Hans J. Vos
University of Twente

ABSTRACT

The purpose of this paper is to design rules for determining the optimal number of interrogatory examples for concept-learning in the Minnesota Adaptive Instructional System (MAIS). It will first be indicated how the problem of designing such optimal rules for instructional decision making can be formalized as a problem of Bayesian decision theory. Subsequently, it will be shown how the loss function assumed in MAIS can be improved by using other results from this decision-theoretic approach. It is argued that in many situations the assumed threshold loss function in MAIS is an unrealistic representation of the loss actually incurred. In view of this, a linear utility function is proposed. It turns out that, the optimal sequential decision rule takes a rather simple form. Moreover, it is assumed that the psychometric model relating observed test scores to the true level of functioning can be represented by Kelley's regression line from classical test theory instead of the binomial model as has been done in MAIS. Finally, some new lines of research are suggested arising from the application of decision theory to the MAIS model.

INTRODUCTION

The term "adaptive instruction" has been in widespread use for over a decade (Farley, 1983; Hansen, Ross & Rakow, 1977; Holland, 1977; Landa, 1976; Park, 1982; Tennyson & Breuer, 1984). Although different authors have defined the term in a different way, most agree that it denotes the use of strategies to adapt instructional treatments to the changing nature of student abilities and characteristics during the learning process (Tennyson & Park,

1984). In the context of computer-based instruction (CBI), adaptive instructional programs are often qualified as individualized study systems (ISS). Examples are the Pittsburgh Individually Prescribed Instruction (IPI) project (Glaser, 1968) and Computer-Assisted Instruction (CAI) (Atkinson, 1968; Suppes, 1966).

In a special JCBI issue on Educational Research and Computer-Based Instruction, Tennyson, Christensen and Park (1984) describe a computer-based adaptive instructional system, the Minnesota Adaptive Instructional System (MAIS). The authors consider MAIS as an intelligent CBI-system, because it exhibits some machine intelligence, as demonstrated by its ability to improve decision making over the history of the system as a function of accumulated information about previous students. In the literature, successful research projects on MAIS have been reported (e.g., Park & Tennyson, 1980; Tennyson, Tennyson & Rothen, 1980).

Initial work on MAIS began as an attempt to design an adaptive instructional strategy for concept-learning (Tennyson, 1975). According to Merrill and Tennyson (1977) concept-learning can be conceived as a two-stage process of formation of conceptual knowledge and development of procedural knowledge (for a complete review of the theory of concept-learning, see Tennyson & Cocchiarella, 1986).

In MAIS, eight basic instructional design variables directly related to specific learning processes are distinguished. In order to adapt instruction to individual learner differences (aptitudes, prior knowledge) and learning needs (amount and sequence of instruction), these variables are controlled by an intelligent tutor system (Tennyson & Christensen, 1986). Three out of these eight variables are directly managed by a computer-based decision strategy.

The purpose of this paper is to review the application of the MAIS decision procedure by Tennyson and his associates. First, it will be indicated how this procedure can be situated within the general framework of (empirical) Bayesian decision theory (e.g., DeGroot, 1970; Ferguson, 1967; Keeney & Raiffa, 1976; Lindgren, 1976), and what implicit assumptions have to be made in doing so.

Using a Bayesian approach, the decision component in MAIS can be improved. As an example, it will be shown how one of the basic elements needed for decisionmaking according to the Bayesian viewpoint can be improved by using other results from decision theory. A linear utility function is proposed to replace the threshold loss function assumed in MAIS. Moreover, optimal sequential decision rules will be derived using Kelley's regression line from classical test theory as the psychometric model instead of the binomial model assumed in MAIS.

The paper concludes with a discussion of some new lines of research arising from the application of decision theory to the MAIS model. We shall confine ourselves in this paper only to one of the three instructional design variables directly managed by the decision component in MAIS, namely determining the optimal number of interrogatory examples (question form).

A FRAMEWORK OF BAYESIAN DECISION THEORY

The derivation of an optimal strategy with respect to the number of interrogatory examples in a concept-learning lesson requires an instructional problem be stated in a form amenable to decision-theoretic analysis. Analyses based on decision theory vary somewhat from field to field, but the following formal elements can be found in most of them:

(1)   A nonempty set, Θ, of possible states of nature.
(2)   A nonempty set, Ω, of actions available to the decision-maker.
(3)   A loss function, $l(a,\theta)$, i.e., a real-valued function defined on $\Omega \times \Theta$.
(4)   A probability function or psychometric model, $f(x|\theta)$, relating observed values x of a stochastic variable X to a given value $\Theta = \theta$ for the state of nature.

These basic elements have been related to decision problems in educational testing by many authors, particularly in the context of computer-based adaptive instructional systems (e.g., Atkinson, 1976; Swaminathan, Hambleton & Algina, 1975; Van der Linden, 1981a). As the use of the decision component in MAIS refers to sequential mastery testing, we shall discuss here only the application of the basic elements to this problem.

The first element concerns the student's true level of functioning $\pi \in [0,1]$. In the present problem, there are two possible states of nature: a student is a true master (θ_1) if his/her true level of functioning exceeds the criterion level $\pi_0 \in [0,1]$, and he/she is a true nonmaster (θ_0) otherwise. The criterion level π_0, the minimum degree of mastery required, is set in advance. Unfortunately, due to measurement and sampling errors, the true level of functioning is unknown. All that is known is the student's observed test score X from a small sample of n interrogatory examples (x = 0,1, ... ,n).

The second element pertains to the following two available actions: advance a student (a_1) to the next concept if his/her test score X exceeds a certain cut-off score c on the observed test score scale X, and retain (a_0) him/her otherwise. Students with test score X below the cut-off score c are provided with additional expository examples (statement form). A new interrogatory example is then generated. This procedure is applied sequentially until either mastery is attained or the pool of test items is exhausted. Now, the sequential mastery decision problem can be stated as choosing a value of c that, given the value of π_0, is optimal in some sense.

The third element describes the loss $l(a_i,\theta_j)$ incurred when action a_i (i=0,1) is taken for the student who is in state θ_j (j=0,1). A loss function specifies the total costs of all possible decision outcomes. These costs concern all relevant psychological, social and economic consequences which the decision brings along. An example of economic consequences is extra computer time associated with presenting additional instructional materials. The loss must be measured on at least an interval scale. In Tennyson's approach the loss function is supposed to be a threshold function. The implicit choice of this function implies that the "seriousness" of all possible consequences of the two available actions can be summarized by four constants, one for each of the four possible decision outcomes (see Table 1).

Table 1
Twofold table for threshold loss function

		True level	
		$\pi \geq \pi_0$ (true master)	$\pi < \pi_0$ (true nonmaster)
Decision	Advance	0	l_{10}
	Retain	l_{01}	0

In Table 1 it is assumed that no losses occur for correct decisions, and that, therefore, the losses associated with correct advance and retain decisions (l_{11} and l_{00}, respectively) can be set equal to zero.

In the decision component of MAIS, a loss ratio R must be specified. R refers to the relative losses associated with advancing a learner whose true level of functioning is below π_0 and retaining one whose true level exceeds π_0. From Table 1 it can be seen that the loss ratio R equals l_{10}/l_{01} for all values of π.

The last element relates the observed test score X to the true level of functioning π. In MAIS this is done by using the binomial model,

$$f(x \mid \pi) = \binom{n}{x} \pi^x (1-\pi)^{n-x}. \tag{1}$$

Within a Bayesian decision-theoretic framework the sequential mastery decision problem is solved by minimizing the "Bayes risk", which is minimal if for each value x of X an action with smallest posterior expected loss is chosen. The posterior expected loss is the expected loss taken with respect to the posterior distribution of π.

It can be seen from the loss table that a decision rule minimizing posterior expected loss is to advance a student whose test score x is such that

$$l_{01}\text{Prob}(\pi \geq \pi_0| x,n) \geq l_{10}\text{Prob}(\pi < \pi_0| x,n), \tag{2}$$

and to retain him/her otherwise. Since $l_{01} > 0$, this is equivalent to advancing a student if

$$\text{Prob}(\pi \geq \pi_0| x,n) \geq R/(1+R), \tag{3}$$

and retaining him/her otherwise. $\text{Prob}(\pi \geq \pi_0| x,n)$ denotes the probability of the student's true level of functioning exceeding π_0, given a test score X on a test of length n. In fact, this probability is given by one minus the cumulative posterior distribution of π. In MAIS this quantity is called the "beta value" or "operating level" (Tennyson, Christensen & Park, 1984).

It should be noted that, as can be seen from the decision rule, the decision-maker need not specify the values of l_{10} and l_{01} completely. He needs only assess their ratio l_{10}/l_{01}. For assessing loss functions, or the more generally applicable utility functions, most texts on decision theory propose lottery methods (see, for example, Luce & Raiffa, 1957, chap. 2; for a recent modification, see Novick & Lindley, 1979). But in principle any psychological scaling method can be used. Although helpful techniques are available, this does not mean that, for example, in programs of individualized instruction, assessment of utilities is always a simple matter. In the next section, we shall consider one method that works in decision problems with a finite number of outcomes such as the sequential mastery decision problem.

In order to initiate the decision component in MAIS, three kinds of parameters must be specified in advance (Rothen & Tennyson, 1984). Beside the parameters π_0 and R, a probability distribution representing the prior knowledge about π must be available. In MAIS, a beta distribution, $B(\alpha,\beta)$, is used as a prior distribution, and a pretest score together with information about other students is used to specify its parameter values.

Keats and Lord (1962) have shown that simple moment estimators for α and β can be derived that are based on the mean, the standard deviation, and the KR-21 reliability coefficient of the test scores from the previous students. Let the KR-21 reliability be defined as

$$\rho XX' = \frac{n}{n-1} [1 - \frac{\mu X(n-\mu X)}{n \sigma^2 X}], \tag{4}$$

where μX and $\sigma^2 X$ denote the mean and the variance of the pretest scores, respectively. Then the estimates $\hat{\alpha}$ and $\hat{\beta}$ of α and β, respectively, are given as

$$\hat{\alpha} = (-1 + 1/\rho XX')\mu X$$

$$\hat{\beta} = -\alpha + n/\rho XX' - n \tag{5}$$

It follows that the posterior distribution of π is easily obtained. From an application of Bayes' theorem, the posterior distribution will again be a member of the beta family (the conjugacy property). In fact, if the prior distribution is $B(\alpha,\beta)$ and the student's test score is x from a test of length n, then the posterior distribution is $B(x+\alpha,n-x+\beta)$. The beta distribution has been extensively tabulated (e.g., Pearson, 1930). Normal approximations are also available (Johnson & Kotz, 1970, sect. 2.4.6). Tennyson and Christensen (1986) use a non-linear regression approach that fits the best polynomial as an approximation of the beta distribution.

The MAIS decision procedure for adapting the number of interrogatory examples can now be summarized as follows: If a student's beta value exceeds the quantity $R/(1+R)$, (s)he is passed to the next instructional unit (i.e., next concept) or final (summative) posttest. However, if his/her beta value is below this quantity, his/her posterior distribution is used as a prior distribution in a next cycle. A new interrogatory example is then generated. The procedure is applied iteratively until either the beta value exceeds the quantity $R/(1+R)$ or all interrogatory examples in the pool for the concept have been presented.

In the next section the choice of the loss function involved in MAIS will be critically reviewed. Subsequently, it will be shown how this function can be improved by using other results from decision theory.

A LINEAR UTILITY FUNCTION

An obvious disadvantage of the threshold utility function is that it assumes constant utility for students to the left or to the right of π_0, no matter how large their distance from π_0. For instance, a misclassified true master with a true level of functioning just above π_0 gives the same utility as a misclassified true master with a true level far above π_0. It seems more realistic to suppose that for misclassified true masters the utility is a monotonically decreasing function of the variable π.

Moreover, as can be seen in Table 1, the threshold utility function shows a "threshold" at the point $\pi = \pi_0$, and this also seems unrealistic in many cases. In the neighbourhood of this point, the utilities for correct and incorrect decisions frequently change smoothly rather than abruptly.

In view of this, Van der Linden and Mellenbergh (1977) propose a linear utility function:

$$u(a_i,\pi) = \begin{cases} b_0(\pi_0-\pi)+d_0 & \text{for retain } (a_0) \\ \\ b_1(\pi-\pi_0)+d_1 & \text{for advance } (a_1) \end{cases} \quad b_0, b_1 > 0 \qquad (6)$$

The above defined function consists of a constant term and a term proportional to the difference between the true level of functioning π and the specified criterion level π_0. The constant amount of utility, d_j (j=0,1), can, for example, represent the utility of testing, which will be mostly negative because costs of testing are involved. The condition b_0, $b_1 > 0$ is equivalent to the statement that for actions a_0 and a_1, utility is a strictly decreasing and increasing function of the variable π, respectively. The parameters b_0, b_1, d_0, and d_1 have to be assessed empirically. Figure 1 displays an example of this function.

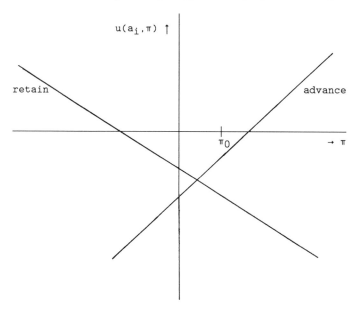

Figure 1. An example of a linear utility function.
$(b_0 \neq b_1, d_0 \neq d_1)$

The linear utility function seems to be a realistic representation of the utilities actually incurred in many decision making situations. In a recent study, for example, it was shown by Van der Gaag (1987) that many empirical utility structures could be approximated by linear functions.

As the general linear utility function now stands, we need to determine the four constants b_0, b_1, d_0, and d_1 before it can be applied. However, if we use the fact that a utility function needs to be determined only up to a positive multiplicative and additive constant (e.g., Luce & Raiffa, 1957), we can reduce the number of unknown constants to two. Thus, since $b_1 > 0$, we may redefine $u(a_i,\pi)$ by making the positive linear transformation $u^*(a_i,\pi) = [u(a_i,\pi)-d_1]/b_1$. And so

$$u^*(a_i,\pi) = \begin{cases} b^*(\pi_0-\pi)+d^* & \text{for } i = 0 \\ \\ \pi - \pi_0 & \text{for } i = 1, \end{cases} \qquad (7)$$

where $b^* = b_0/b_1$ and $d^* = (d_0-d_1)/b_1$.

We turn now to an illustration of one of the most direct methods available for determining the constants b^* and d^*. In order to make the method work, the decision-maker must be able to specify two ordered pairs (π_i, π_j) and (π_i', π_j') such that

$$u^*(a_0, \pi_i) = u^*(a_1, \pi_j)$$

and   (8)

$$u^*(a_0, \pi_i') = u^*(a_1, \pi_j').$$

Solving this system of equations, we find that

$$b^* = (\pi_j - \pi_j')/(\pi_i' - \pi_i) \text{ and } d^* = \pi_j - \pi_0 - b^*(\pi_0 - \pi_i).$$ (9)

Since the π-coordinate of the intersection of both utility lines $u^*(a_0, \pi)$ and $u^*(a_1, \pi)$ may be chosen as one of the ordered pairs, it follows that

$$b^* = (\pi_j - \pi_p)/(\pi_p - \pi_i)$$
                                                                                         (10)
$$d^* = (\pi_p - \pi_0)(1 + b^*),$$

where π_p denotes the point of intersection.

Analogous to the minimization of posterior expected loss, decision theory with a utility function requires us to select that action which will maximize the posterior expected utility. So, the decision rule that maximizes the posterior expected utility in the case of a linear utility function is to advance a student with test score x for which

$$E[(\pi - \pi_0)| x, n] \geq E[b^*(\pi_0 - \pi) + d^*| x, n],$$ (11)

and to retain him/her otherwise. Since $(1 + b^*) > 0$, this is equivalent to advancing a student if

$$E[\pi| x, n] \geq \pi_0 + d^*/(1 + b^*),$$ (12)

and retaining him/her otherwise. In other words, with linear utility, the action taken depends only upon the expectation of the posterior distribution of π, other attributes of the distribution are irrelevant for decision purposes.

Using the fact that the expectation of a beta distribution $B(\alpha, \beta)$ is equal to $\alpha/(\alpha+\beta)$, and, thus, the posterior expectation equals $(\alpha+x)/(\alpha+x+\beta+n-x)$, it follows that a student is advanced if his/her test score x is such that

$$x \geq [\alpha+\beta+n][\pi_0 + d^*/(1+b^*)] - \alpha,$$ (13)

and retained otherwise.

Putting $u^*(a_0,\pi)$ and $u^*(a_1,\pi)$ equal to each other, it appears that the π-coordinate of the intersection of both utility lines from Formula (7), π_p, is equal to $\pi_0+d^*/(1+b^*)$. Therefore, the decision rule can be viewed as advancing a student if his/her expectation of the posterior distribution of π is to the right of the intersection point, and retaining him/her otherwise. Note that with linear utility, only the point of intersection, π_p, of the two functions for retain and advance are needed, and, thus the intercept and slope from Formula (7) does not have to be estimated. Hence, expression 13 is equivalent to

$$x \geq [\alpha + \beta + n] \, \pi_p - \alpha. \tag{14}$$

When $d^* = 0$, that is, $d_0 = d_1$, both utility lines intersect at $\pi = \pi_0$ and an interesting case arises. Then, all utility function parameters vanish from the decision rule and, thus, it takes the form of advancing a student if

$$E[\pi| x,n] \geq \pi_0, \tag{15}$$

and retaining him/her otherwise. In other words, if the amounts of constant utility, d_j, for both decisions are equal, or if there are no constant utilities at all, then there is no need to assess the parameters d^* and b^* in adapting the number of interrogatory examples. In that case, the decision rule can even be simplified to advance a student if his/her expectation of the posterior distribution of π is greater than or equal to the specified criterion level p_0, and to retain him/her otherwise.

The expectation of the posterior distribution, $E[\pi| x,n]$, represents the regression of π on x. A possible regression function is the linear regression function of classical test theory (Lord & Novick, 1968):

$$E[\pi| x,n] = \rho_{XX'}\frac{x}{n} + (1-\rho_{XX'})\frac{\mu_X}{n}. \tag{16}$$

Equation 16 is known as Kelley's regression line. This is an interesting equation in that it expresses the estimate of true score as a weighted sum of two separated estimates-one based upon the student's observed score, X, and, the other based upon the mean, μ_X, of the group to which s(he) belongs. If the test is highly reliable, much weight is given to the test score and little to the group mean, and vice versa.

Substituting Equation 16 into expression 15, and solving for x gives the following optimal sequential decision rule

$$x \geq \mu_X + \frac{n \{\pi_0 + d^*/(1+b^*)\} - \mu_X}{\rho_{XX'}}. \tag{17}$$

If the amounts of constant utility for both decisions are equal, i.e. $d^* = 0$, or if there are no constant utilities at all, expression 17 will take the rather simple form

$$x \geq \mu X + \frac{n\pi_0 - \mu X}{\rho XX'} = \frac{\mu X(\rho XX'-1) + n\pi_0}{\rho XX'}. \tag{18}$$

Since $0 \leq \rho XX' \leq 1$, and, thus $-1 \leq \rho XX'-1 \leq 0$, it follows from (18) that μX and the optimal sequential cutting score, x, are related negatively. The higher the average performance, the lower the optimal sequential cutting score. Hard-working students are rewarded by low cutting scores, while less hard-working students will just be penalized and confronted with high cutting scores. This is the opposite of what happens when norm-referenced standards are used (Van der Linden & Mellenbergh, 1987).

It should be stressed that, since the optimal sequential cutting score depends upon μX and $\rho XX'$, as can be seen from (17), the decision component in MAIS allows for an updating after each response to an interrogatory example. This explains why, though the decisions for determining the optimal number of interrrogatory examples are made with respect to an individual student, the rules for the decisons are based on data from all students taught by the system in the past and, in doing so, are improved continuously. In other words, an adaptive instructional system can be designed in this way, i.e., a system of rules improving itself over the history of the system as a result of systematically using accumulated data from previous students.

NEW LINES OF RESEARCH

There are a few new lines of research arising from the application of decision theory to the decision component in MAIS. The first is the extension of the work of Tennyson and his associates to situations where guessing and carelessness are incorporated. Morgan (1979) has developed a model with corrections for guessing and carelessness within a Bayesian decision-theoretic framework. The results of a computer simulation of the model indicate that guessing and carelessness may markedly affect the determination of cutting scores, and hence the accuracy of decisions about mastery.

The second line is research into other prior distributions for π (for example, the standard normal distribution) than the beta distribution assumed in MAIS. It might also be assumed that no prior distribution about π is available, because specifying such a distribution is too difficult a job to accomplish. In these circumstances, the minimax procedure may be an appropriate framework (e.g., Huynh, 1980; Van der Linden, 1981b) which requires no prior distribution regarding the true level of functioning. In this case, the optimum cutting score is obtained by minimizing the maximum risk which would incurred by misclassifications.

Finally, an interesting new line of research seems to be an extension of the action space Ω. In MAIS, two actions were available to the decision-maker, namely advancing (a_1) or retaining (a_0) a student. However, it might also be assumed that there are three (or any finite number) of actions open to the decision-maker. For example, in the three-action problem the student may be provided with additional instructional materials both of the present and the previous concept (a_2); (s)he may be provided only with additional instructional materials of the present concept (a_0); or, (s)he may advance to the next concept (a_1).

We might think of this problem in terms of specifying two cutting scores c_0 and c_1 on the observed test score scale X, where $c_0 < c_1$. Then for observed test score $X < c_0$, action a_2 will be taken; for $c_0 < X < c_1$, action a_0 will be taken; and, for $X > c_1$, action a_1 will be taken.

Davis, Hickman and Novick (1973) have given a solution to the three-action problem using a natural extension of the threshold loss function. Although the notation becomes more complex and the computation a bit more tedious, there are no fundamentally new ideas in the multiple-action problem.

SOME CONCLUDING REMARKS

In this paper it was indicated how the MAIS decision procedure could be formalized within a Bayesian decision-theoretic framework. In fact, it turned out that this decision could be considered as a sequential mastery decision.

Moreover, it was argued that in many situations the assumed threshold loss function in MAIS is an unrealistic representation of the loss actually incurred. Instead, a linear utility function was proposed to meet the objections to threshold loss.

Whether or not the proposed linear utility function instead of the assumed threshold loss function is, however, really an improvement of the present decision component in MAIS (in terms of student performance on posttests, learning time, and amount of instruction) must be decided on the basis of empirical data.

Note

The author is indebted to Wim J. van der Linden for his valuable comments on earlier drafts of the paper.

REFERENCES

Atkinson, R.C. (1968). Computer-based instruction in initial reading. In *Proceedings of the 1967 Invitational Conference on Testing Problems*. Princeton, NJ: Educational Testing Service.

Atkinson, R.C. (1976). Adaptive instructional systems: Some attempts to optimize the learning process. In D. Klahr (Ed.), *Cognition and instruction*. New York: John Wiley & Sons.

Davis, C.E., Hickman, J., & Novick, M.R. (1973). *A primer on decision analysis for individually prescribed instruction* (ACT Technical Bulletin No. 17). Iowa City, IA: The American College Testing Program.

DeGroot, M.H. (1970). *Optimal statistical decisions*. New York: McGraw-Hill.

Farley, F.H. (1981). Basic process individual differences: A biologically based theory of individualization for cognitive, affective, and creative outcomes. In F.H. Farley & N.J. Gordon (Eds.), *Psychology and education: The state of the union*. Berkeley, CA: McCutchan, 9-29.

Ferguson, T.S. (1967). *Mathematical statistics: A decision theoretic approach*. New York: Academic Press.

Glaser, R. (1968). Adapting the elementary school curriculum to individual performance. In *Proceedings of the 1967 Invitational Conference on Testing Problems*. Princeton, NJ: Educational Testing Service.

Hansen, D.N., Ross, S.M., & Rakow, E. (1977). *Adaptive models for computer-based training systems* (Annual report to Naval Personnel Research and Development Center). Memphis, TN: Memphis State University.

Holland, J.G. (1977). Variables in adaptive decisions in individualized instruction. *Educational Psychologist, 12*, 146-161.

Huynh, H. (1980). A nonrandomized minimax solution for passing scores in the binomial error model. *Psychometrika, 45,* 167-182.

Johnson, N.L., & Kotz, S. (1970). *Distributions in statistics: Continuous univariate distributions - 2*. Boston: Houghton Mifflin.

Keats, J.A., & Lord, F.M. (1962). A theoretical distribution for mental test scores. *Psychometrika, 27,* 59-72.

Keeney, D., & Raiffa, H. (1976). *Decisions with multiple objectives: Preferences and value trade-offs*. New York: John Wiley & Sons.

Landa, N.L. (1976). *Instructional regulation and control*. Englewood Cliffs, NJ: Educational Technology Publications.

Lindgren, B.W. (1976). *Statistical theory* (3rd ed.). New York: Macmillan.

Lord, F.M., & Novick, M.R. (1968). *Statistical theories of mental test scores*. Reading, M.A.: Addison Wesley.

Luce, R.D., & Raiffa, H. (1957). *Games and decisions*. New York: John Wiley & Sons.

Merrill, M.D., & Tennyson, R.D. (1977). *Teaching concepts: An instructional design guide*. Englewood Cliffs, NJ: Educational Technology Publications.

Morgan, G. (1979). *A criterion-referenced measurement model with corrections for guessing and carelessness* (Occasional Paper No. 13). Victoria: The Australian Council for Educational Research Limited.

Novick, M.R., & Lindley, D.V. (1979). Fixed-state assessment of utility functions. *Journal of the American Statistical Association, 74,* 306-311.

Park, O. (1982). A response-sensitive strategy in computer-based instruction. *Journal of Educational Technology Systems, 10,* 187-197.

Park, O., & Tennyson, R.D. (1980). Adaptive design strategies for selecting number and presentation order of examples in coordinate concept acquisition. *Journal of Educational Psychology, 72,* 362-370.

Pearson, K. (1930). *Tables for statisticians and biometricians, 2,* London: Cambridge University Press.

Suppes, P. (1966). The use of computers in education. *Scientific American, 215,* 206-221.

Swaminathan, H., Hambleton, R.K., & Algina, J. (1975). A Bayesian decision-theoretic procedure for use with criterion-referenced tests. *Journal of Educational Measurement, 12,* 87-98.

Tennyson, R.D. (1975). Adaptive instructional models for concept acquisition. *Educational Technology, 15*(4), 7-15.

Tennyson, R.D., & Breuer, K. (1984). Cognitive-based design guidelines for using video and computer technology in higher education. In O. Zuber-Sherritt (Ed.), *Video in higher education.* London, England: Kogan Page Ltd., 26-630.

Tennyson, R.D., Christensen, D.L., & Park, S.I. (1984). The Minnesota Adaptive Instructional System: An intelligent CBI system. *Journal of Computer-Based Instruction, 11,* 2-13.

Tennyson, R.D., & Christensen, D.L. (1986). MAIS: An intelligent learning system. In D. Jonassen (Ed.), *Instructional designs for microcomputer courseware.* Hillsdale, NJ: Lawrence Erlbaum Associates.

Tennyson, R.D., & Cocchiarella, M.J. (1986). An empirically based instructional design theory for teaching concepts. *Review of Educational Research, 56*(1), 40-71.

Tennyson, R.D., & Park, O. (1984). Computer-based adaptive instructional systems: A review of empirically based models. *Machine-Mediated Learning, 1,* 129-153.

Tennyson, C.L., Tennyson, R.D., & Rothen, W. (1980). Content structure and management strategies as design variables in concept acquisition. *Journal of Educational Psychology, 72,* 499-505.

Van der Gaag, N.L. (1987). *Applications of empirical linear utility functions to mastery decisions.* Paper presented at the European Psychometric Society, Enschede, The Netherlands.

Van der Linden, W.J. (1981a). Using aptitude measurements for the optimal assignment of subjects to treatments with and without mastery scores. *Psychometrika, 46,* 257-274.

Van der Linden, W.J. (1981b). Decision models for use with criterion-referenced tests. *Applied Psychological Measurement, 4,* 469-492.

Van der Linden, W.J., & Mellenbergh, G.J. (1977). Optimal cutting scores using a linear loss function. *Applied Psychological Measurement, 1,* 593-599.

12

THE DESCRIPTION OF KNOWLEDGE AND SKILLS FOR THE PURPOSE OF INSTRUCTION

Sanne Dijkstra
University of Twente

ABSTRACT

In this chapter the structure of knowledge for the purpose of designing instruction is described. First different descriptions of knowledge which are developed by instructional designers are reviewed and integrated in a new subject matter categorization system. Then the skills which are related with the knowledge are specified and the necessary student activity is shown. Finally the implications for instructional design are made clear. Attention is paid to the synchronization of the training of a skill and the acquisition of knowledge. The content of previous chapters is used and illustrated.

INTRODUCTION

The goal of education is the transition of knowledge and skills to people, who can use these for understanding reality, making predictions, anticipating events and for doing their jobs.

In Western culture the realization of that goal takes the student a long time, generally 12 years compulsory attendance in elementary and high school. Usually people try to finish their education with vocational training, which is a condition for getting a job. Doing their jobs means being engaged in activities which are pertinent for that profession or trade. These activities are situated in the community in which people live and are purposeful. An adequate vocational training program engages the student in those activities, which promote the acquisition of the knowledge and skills of that field.

About two centuries ago students generally attended elementary school for a few years to learn a number of basic skills, e.g. reading and writing. Afterwards most of them either went to work or became apprentices of a guild, later novices and finally experts. The industrial revolution and the French revolution gradually changed the guild system. The guilds no longer were able to adequately cover the increasing number of types of jobs. The governments regulated the extension of the number of elementary school years and founded high schools. Gradually in the 19th century the system of primary and secondary education developed, which took on its typical features: the splitting up of knowledge and skills into subjects; the definition of educational and behavioral goals for these subjects state- or nationwide; the definition of standards based on which the students' achievement is evaluated; provision of an extra year for students who do not meet the standards or referring the student to a class having a less demanding goal; instruction by one teacher for a class of 20 to 30 students; abstraction of knowledge from the situation or subculture where it is used for solving problems to a body of knowledge which often is transmitted orally to a group of students; and, finally, homework for the students to rehearse the knowledge and train the skills.

It has become commonplace to bemoan this system because its features are often considered to be disadvantageous for learning to solve real problems. In addition, the system is seen as one that encourages competition among students for the best grades instead of real interest in the subject matter (Nicholls, 1984).

It doesn't help elementary and high school teachers a lot to criticize the system within which they are working and to question the effectiveness of their instructional methods without offering indications as to what to do to possibly overcome the problems. Of course the same applies for instructions in other schools and training departments.

In a recent paper, Brown, Collins and Duguid (1988) criticize the notion of knowledge as a substance which can be transmitted to students. Instead they stress the idea that knowledge is *constructed* by students as a result of being involved in authentic activity. This means, activity of practitioners endorsed explicitly or implicitly by members of the subculture. Authentic activity gives the learner "access to the perceptual standpoint that enables practitioners to understand what they do" and contributes to the formation of the representation of the problem situation, because the learner is actually engaged in the problem situation. To see a blueprint of a machine is different from seeing the machine itself. And this is different from acting upon and repairing the machine. The latter activity is authentic. It results in perceptions from actions and it is this activity that shapes the learning process and helps to construct the representation. Brown, Collins and Duguid label this representation indexical which means that it is dependent on the context. Indexicals are words like I, you, here, now, this, from there, etc. The possible and meaningful use of these indexicals in a conversation relies on the hearer's access to the real problem situation, not in observing its blueprint or other representational diagram, except in case drawing a diagram is part of solving a design problem.

The idea of the construction of knowledge by students, who later can use this knowledge as tools for solving problems and making predictions, suggests a need for integrating the development of knowledge and the acquisition of skills. This point of view usually will be confirmed by teachers and instructors, but their question then will be how to design the instruction which will cause or promote the joint integration. The design of this instruction depends on the examples chosen, the sequence of words used in the instructional statements, the sequence of the statements themselves, the activity shown to and asked of the students, and the questions or problems asked. All this should be done in such a way that the student is active. Being active means manipulating the "objects" involved, classifying and changing them and making predictions. In doing so the student is making errors and wrong predictions. These experiences are the conditions for modifying existent knowledge and thus constructing new knowledge.

It now becomes clear that the description of knowledge, its structure and its representation in memory is essential for designing instruction. The instructor has to know this and be able to design instruction such that the student is able to construct the knowledge based on his/her actions. This means further that instructional design theories and models should help the teachers/instructors to recognize which knowledge is involved, how it is structured and what to do with this "meta-knowledge" in guiding and accompanying the students' actions in constructing their knowledge. In instructional design theories, however, the description of knowledge is complicated and sometimes confusing. What are facts, concrete concepts, rules, principles, higher order rules, procedures, declarative-, procedural- and causal knowledge? What is knowledge about objects and about cognitive operations? What is process knowledge and how can teachers promote the construction of it by students?

In this article the structure of knowledge and skills will be discussed, then its implications for designing instruction will be addressed.

KNOWLEDGE AND SKILLS AS DEFINED BY GAGNE AND BRIGGS

The expected outcome of instruction as described by Gagné, Briggs and Wager (1988) is learned behavior or a learned capability. There are five categories of learning outcomes: intellectual skills, cognitive strategies, verbal information, motor skills and attitudes. Intellectual skills are further classified into discrimination, concrete and defined concepts, rules and higher order rules. This enumeration shows there is no typical distinction between knowledge and skills. However Gagné, Briggs and Wager explicitly use the word *knowledge* and *body of knowledge* when they describe verbal information, also labeled verbal knowledge and declarative knowledge. This latter information is learned by "school instruction" or from the reading of books, magazines, newspapers, and by way of radio and television programs.

An intellectual skill is a skill for doing something of an intellectual sort. The categories of intellectual skills mentioned are shown in Figure 1.

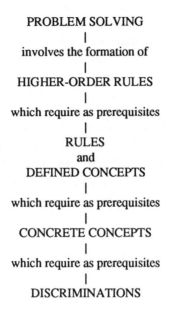

PROBLEM SOLVING
|
involves the formation of
|
HIGHER-ORDER RULES
|
which require as prerequisites
|
RULES
and
DEFINED CONCEPTS
|
which require as prerequisites
|
CONCRETE CONCEPTS
|
which require as prerequisites
|
DISCRIMINATIONS

Figure 1. Levels of complexity in intellectual skills (from Gagné, Briggs & Wager, 1988).

They will be described shortly. A discrimination is a capability of making different responses to stimuli which differ from each other along one or more physical dimensions. The response is required to show that the discrimination is learned. A concrete concept is a capability to recognize a concrete object as a member of a category, based on a perceptible object property. There is no definition acquired. The student can label the object and point to it. Examples of objects being categorized in this way are "ball", "house", etc. If a defined concept is learned the learner has the capability to classify a particular object, event or relation. The act of classification is based on a definition which describes the "meaning" of a particular class of objects. Gagné and Briggs also label this definition a classifying rule. The application of a rule, however, implies more than a classifying rule. Rules also include relationships like "equal to", "greater than", "less than", etc. Moreover principles of science which are learned by the student are described as rule-using behavior. Gagné, Briggs and Wager give the example of F= ma. The rule embodied in this statement can be applied in solving the problem: "What will be the acceleration of a body of 5 kilograms when acted on by a force of 3 Newtons?"

Finally a higher order rule is defined, which is a combination of simpler rules to solve a problem. Often the rule is invented by the student; it is constructed by using simpler rules. If this happens with no guidance or with a minimal amount of guidance, then the rule is discovered and that makes the learning a problem-solving event.

The introduction of intellectual skills as a capability, together with verbal information as another class of learning outcomes, makes it difficult to clearly distinguish between knowledge and skills. In the acts of discrimination and categorization of objects, for example, both knowledge and skills are involved. Because Gagné, Briggs and Wager define concepts and rules as intellectual skills, the difference between knowledge and skills is obscured. This will be discussed in more detail later.

KNOWLEDGE AND SKILLS AS DEFINED BY MERRILL

Being aware that a one-dimensional classification system, which was originally proposed by Gagné (1965), was too limited for the description of different categories of learning outcomes, Merrill and Boutwell (1973) proposed a two-dimensional classification system. One dimension (labeled content) was partitioned into paired associate, concept, principle and problem. The other dimension retained the original capabilities defined by Gagné, namely discrimination, classification, rule using and higher order rule using. Later, Merrill (1983) revised the two-dimensional classification system in what became known as the performance-content matrix. From Figure 2 it can be seen that there are four types of content (fact, concept, procedure and principle) and that there are three levels of performance (remember, use and find). Recently Merrill (1987) changed his instructional design theory and related prescriptive rules for the actual design of instruction in the component design theory, but this new theory retains the two-dimensional classification system for instructional outcomes. The categories, however, are elaborated to provide more detailed classification. Content types are expanded to content structures which include lists, taxonomies (parts of ..., kinds of ...), algorithms (for procedures such as calculation and assembly), event chains (for natural processes like life cycles) and causal chains. Merrill further describes the kinds taxonomy in this volume.

Again it is not completely clear how the authors distinguish between knowledge and skills. If knowledge comprises facts, concept and principles, and the use of procedures are skills, then the question whether there is a clear distinction between knowledge and skills still cannot be answered. The examples given by Merrill (1983) make clear that at the use and find levels of concept a classification skill is supposed. The same applies for the principle level.

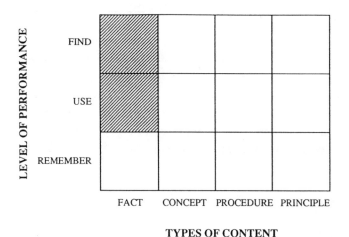

Figure 2. Performance-content matrix (from Merrill, 1983).

THE DESCRIPTION OF KNOWLEDGE AND SKILLS BY LANDA

Landa (1983) makes a clear distinction between knowledge and skills and emphasizes the interconnectedness. The learning and practicing of skills require knowledge.

In Landa's description of knowledge and skills the object is paramount. Knowledge of objects emerges in three forms: First as a perceptive image (a person can watch an object); second, as a mental image of an object (a representation which is available even though the object is not actually present); and third, as a concept (a form of knowledge that represents an object as "a set of its characteristic features"). A concept can be expressed as a proposition. However this is not necessary, because a person can have a correct concept of an object, but may not be able to give a correct definition of it. Other knowledge about objects, e.g. its relations with other objects, are formulated as propositions, Thus definitions, axioms, postulates, laws and rules are propositions.

A skill, Landa states, is an ability to apply knowledge. A skill manifests itself in special actions on objects, or their representations. These actions are operations. Motor or material operations transform material objects, whereas cognitive operations are those operations that transform the mental representation of objects, both images and concepts. Moreover, propositions can be transformed, which also means transformations of laws, rules and so on.

Finally Landa offers a definition of a process which is a functioning system of operations, e.g. a production process. Sometimes the word procedure is used but this label doesn't have a formal description in Landa's theory of instruction, because it can be used for one singular individual problem, without referring to a general system of operations.

SYNTHESIS AND EXTENSION

The description of knowledge and skills for purposes of instruction thus far shows some differences. The existing differences, however, are not of use for instructional designers. Moreover, it remains unclear how the construction of knowledge is dependent upon and interacts with the activity in learning a skill.

Hereafter the differences will be addressed and a description of knowledge and skills will be presented. The labels used are declarative, procedural and causal knowledge, which are borrowed from Anderson (1982, 1988). A distinction between the description of static and dynamic situations and their interdependencies will be made. Further, the use of existing knowledge and skills will be separated from the construction of new knowledge and skills, as in scientific experiments.

Knowledge is defined as the internal or external representation of objects and their lawful relationships. Skill is the ability to use the knowledge effectively and readily in solving both well- and ill-defined problems.

The construction of knowledge interacts with the learning of a skill. Once the basic knowledge is constructed, generalization is possible and unlimited amounts of conceptual knowledge can be acquired. For instance, learning to read a map is a skill which is gradually developing. A nine year old child learns to draw and use a plan of his/her classroom, e.g. the child marks his/her chair. Then a plan of the school and schoolyard is drawn. The scale is checked by walking along its borders and measuring their lengths. Further a part of the city area or the village involved is either drawn or shown. The child marks his/her home and the kids walk an itinerary. Later road maps and other maps of states and nations are presented. Once the skill of reading a local map is developed it generalizes to reading a map of any area in the world. The skill of reading the symbols of a legend makes clear which knowledge can be abstracted. The reading shows the location of industries, forests, lakes, oceans, villages and towns, roads connecting them, and so on. This means that the knowledge it represents is meaningful and possibly can be represented in memory. The instruction first is at a do level. Draw (or copy) a plan, mark your seat and so on.

The instruction has a clear object to describe: the classroom, the school. The activity refers to its structure and parts. This stage of instruction is elaborate. It requires abstraction from the real situation. The whole and its parts are labeled, the symbols are presented and copied. This is the declarative stage as described by Anderson (1982). The knowledge involved refers to facts. "This is a plan of our classroom". "A line represents a wall". "One centimeter represents one meter", and so on. Later the conceptual level is reached. Both class and relational concepts are constructed and represented. For instance in further reading a map, a village of under 500 inhabitants is shown by a black dot. A village of 500 to 2500 inhabitants is shown by a small open circle and a village of 2500 to 5000 by a black dot in an open circle. Construction of conceptual knowledge in this example means that a class concept "a village is a community of up to 5000 inhabitants" is acquired.

In the same way relational concepts are constructed. "Syracuse is located in New York". "Philadelphia is located in Pennsylvania". These facts generalize to "a city is located in a state". In this way more relations between cities and states as identifiable "objects" are developed, e.g. ... is the capital of ..., ... is the biggest city in .... And relations between cities are developed: ... is at 20 mile distance from ..., ... is across the river from ..., ... is north from ....

The construction of the knowledge is supported by instruction, both expository and inquisitory. Thus the instructor makes a statement like: "Often you will find a city located at a river". And: "Can you show me on which river Philadelphia is located?"

Thus far, the kinds of knowledge involved are facts and concepts, both class and relational. The formal description is given underneath.

Class concepts

Consider the following incomplete proposition: x is a positive number. It is impossible to conclude whether the proposition is true or false, because x, a variable, has no value. Changing the variable to a constant, 3 is a positive number makes the conclusion possible. The nature of the proposition refers to class and relational concepts. A class concept ascribes an object to a category. It is a description, based on which an object is placed in a category. The incomplete proposition which in principle refers to objects, has one variable. Consider the following expressions: The class of all objects x, such that x is ... On the dotted line a feature of the object will be written. And consider the expression: The object x is an element of the category K. To make it concrete: The set (class, category) of all numbers, such that $x > 0$. This is the set of positive numbers. And: The number 3 is an element of the set of positive numbers. It is assumed that an incomplete proposition with only one variable fulfills only one class with elements, those and only those objects that meet the condition.

Relational concepts

A relation or relational concept is a description of the correspondence between ordered pairs of objects. Relations order objects, sometimes sequence them. In the form of an incomplete proposition the expression has two or more variables. The general form of the expression is The object x has the relation R to the object y. Of course a negation is possible. For two individual objects, x is labeled the *predecessor* and y the *successor*. The predecessor is an element of a set, which is labeled the *domain*. The successor is also an element of a set, labeled the *range*. Domain and range can be the same set. With relational concepts, all kinds of relations between human beings are described. For example, a is the father of b, a has power over b, etc. Relations of general significance are the *identity* and the *equivalence* relation. Further the functional relation y= f(x) and its specializations: the sequence and the series.

It is assumed that every incomplete proposition with two variables x and y fulfills a specific relation existing between the objects x and y, if and only if the objects meet the relation stated in the incomplete proposition.

It is supposed that the knowledge about facts is represented in memory as a network of propositions (Stillings, Feinstein, Garfield, Rissland, Rosenbaum, Weisler & Baker-Ward, 1987). The network also can contain general propositions, such as "Streets are drawn by lines". The cluster of general propositions, which are attached either to one or to two or more concept nodes are labeled a conceptual schema. The schemas are abstractions, which allow people to assign particular objects to general categories or to specify general relations between objects.

The knowledge about facts and the conceptual knowledge together constitute the body of declarative knowledge.

As stated before, the learning of a skill and the construction of knowledge interact. The instruction temporarily can be directed to knowledge acquisition, or to parts of a skill, but the development of one of these processes in isolation may become meaningless. The expert skill of using a map first means being able to identify the information based on conceptual knowledge. The identification means that villages, towns, roads, etc. can be categorized and their locations found. For example, using the index for cities, Wichita (KS.) and Wichita (TX.) have to be found. The procedure for doing this has a number of steps or identification operations, which are enumerated in a production system (Anderson, 1982). These operations together constitute the identification algorithm, which is a skill. The mental representation of this skill is labeled procedural knowledge. The skill is a procedure for solving the problem. If I have to visit this city, where is this city? To solve the problem the operationalized relationship or fact "Wichita" is located in "Kansas" is used. The procedure involves a number of productions, such as:

IF
    the location of Wichita (KS) has to be found
THEN
    the Kansas State map is necessary
IF
    Kansas State map is available
THEN
    read the index of cities and find the coordinates.

Procedures for finding a location are numerous and sometimes detailed, for example the procedures, which together are labeled position by dead reckoning for navigation at sea. In this situation at least two relations are necessary to locate an object. "This ship is located at the intersection of 4° 11' 35'' E and 53° 15' 23'' N. Further, the relationship between parallels and meridians in geography is required. Knowledge is constructed with the help of instruction from perceptions and from data. This construction happens by doing (in a problem solving process).

The operations or problem solving procedure to construct the knowledge can become complicated. What, for example, is the procedure to find the functional relationship $y = 1/2 \ x^2 + 1/2 \ x$, if the natural numbers are the domain and the positive numbers (1, 3, 6, 10, 15, ...) are the range?

Thus far knowledge and skills are described for static situations. The object does not change. Table 1 shows the main categories in their simple form. In complex forms conceptual structures are distinguished. This can be both class conceptual structures and structures of relational concepts or combinations of them.

An example of a class conceptual structure is a taxonomy, of a relational conceptual structure a family tree.

Table 1
Declarative and causal knowledge, related problems and procedural knowledge (skills)

Declarative knowledge	Problem	Procedural knowledge
Fact	What is the name of this single symbol, object, event?	Recognition
Concept		
class concept	To which category does this object belong?	Identification operations, Categorization
relational concept	What is the relationship between these objects?	Identification operations Application of problem-solving procedures

Causal knowledge	Problem	Procedural knowledge
Condition and biconditions (series of events, process, causal chain)	What will happen after a certain time lapse?	Making predictions by application of the lawful relationships

Meta knowledge	Problem	Procedural Knowledge
Plans, strategies	How to plan, how to attack a problem?	Thinking skills

Objects and situations change based on the principles of nature or are transformed because people perform operations on them. A transformation is caused by performing one or more operations on the object. Mathematical "objects" are changed by applying mathematical operations. Usually a "system of operations" is performed on an object, which defines a series of changes, labeled a process. Such processes comprise many different operations on different objects, these being the parts of new objects, which, for example is the case in a production process.

The changes of objects and situations are described in a series of events, production processes and causal chains. A closer look at the description shows that class and relational concepts are basic for the description of the objects and its relationships, which are involved in the process. These class and relational concepts therefore are sometimes labeled the vehicles of thinking. The change of the objects or situations involved is described in conditional and biconditional statements, which sometimes take on the form of laws.

Chains of events and causal chains are supposed to be represented in memory in scripts (Schank and Abelson, 1977) and qualitative process models (Anderson, 1988). The knowledge of series of events, processes and causal chains is constructed by questioning the data and making inferences. The knowledge is changed by making wrong predictions about what will happen in a certain process or in a certain situation.

A prediction involves both knowledge and skill. To make this point of view clear a few problems will be discussed.

First, suppose I am living in Syracuse and wish to visit a relative in Pittsburgh. If I leave at 10 a.m. how late will I arrive, being able to drive at an average speed of 45 miles an hour? To solve this problem both the knowledge of maps and the skill of reading a map, together with the application of mathematical operations, will make a prediction possible. The knowledge is changed if the actual prediction turns out to be wrong. A wrong prediction can be caused by lack of (parts of the) knowledge and mistakes in the application of operations. What changes in this example is the person's location at a certain time.

Second, for the purpose of instruction, it is sometimes necessary that the instructor deliberately makes wrong predictions. These techniques are part of the instructional dialogue. The wrong predictions are based on the student's incomplete knowledge and are made to support the inference process and knowledge construction (Collins 1977, 1988; Collins, Warnock, Aiello & Miller, 1973). An example. The causal chain describing the process of growing rice reads: If rice is planted (a) and the area is flooded (b) and the soil is fertile (c) and there is a warm temperature (d) then and only then rice will grow (q). This biconditional [$(a \wedge b \wedge c \wedge d) \longleftrightarrow q$] is equivalent to [$q \longleftrightarrow (a \wedge b \wedge c \wedge d)$]. Assume that the concept of plant and the chain of events of a plants life cycle are known by the student. This knowledge makes the dialogue possible. Suppose a student answers the question "Why do they grow rice in China?" by stating: "They have lots of rain to supply water for rice growing". A wrong prediction by the teacher in an inquisitory format now will trigger the knowledge construction process, for example "Do they grow rice in Ireland?" This means that the student will search for another variable which is part of the biconditional. The knowledge will not be modified if there is no external evidence which shows it is wrong or if there is no person who says that it is wrong. A problem arises in case of more ill-defined cause and effect relationships. A wrong prediction does not necessarily involve the modification of knowledge.

A third example of a causal chain of events is an electric circuit. What happens somewhere in the circuit is predicted, based on scientific or theoretical knowledge. This knowledge involves classifications like charge, atoms, neutrons, electrons and relationships between variables of the energy source and the elements of the circuit, such as resistance and conductivity, voltage and ampère. There is a strong perceptual element in the representation of this knowledge (R. Chabay, personal communication, November 25, 1988). The skills related to this knowledge again are the identification of the objects and its features and the prediction of future events, which are made by calculations based on the lawful relationships described in mathematical functions. Central to the acquisition of knowledge is the formulation and testing of hypotheses. This is made possible by experimentation, by using observations and empirical findings in such a way that the knowledge will be constructed systematically; for example, by changing no more then one variable its effect can be made clear. These instructional situations where the student can make predictions and inferences often are labeled discovery worlds and the related learning *discovery learning*.

For conditional and biconditional statements and for the description of series of events, (production)processes and causal chains the label causal knowledge is proposed. The causal knowledge and related skills are shown in Table 1.

Further, meta knowledge is to be distinguished. This involves the knowledge of planning and strategies for addressing a problem, how to practice a skill and rehearse knowledge. It is not further discussed here.

The examples shown thus far make clear the student is active. This is necessary to synchronize the acquisition of the knowledge and the gradual development of the skill. To activate the student the instructor presents problems to the student. Solving the problems means both the acquisition of the knowledge and the development of the problemsolving procedure. The first stage of the learning process, the declarative stage is time consuming and has to be designed carefully. If the student is missing a step or operation, help has to be provided. Once the procedure is learned, compiled and carried out automatically, new, comparable knowledge, which is developed by the same problemsolving procedures, can be presented. Now the student can read the knowledge ("information"), without solving the related problems. In case the knowledge no longer belongs to the same domain, new problems have to be presented. And again the construction of new knowledge and the training of the skill take place concurrently. Because problems are presented the student finds or discovers new "things": names of objects, features of objects and lawful relationships between objects. In case of causal chains and processes,the student tries to describe the regularaties and develops an interpretation. The general type of problem for different kinds of knowledge and skills is described in Table 1.

For a student, to solve problems and discover "things" is not the same process as for a scientist in doing experiments. In instruction, the problems are designed in a systematic way, thus that the student can construct the required knowledge and train the problem-solving procedure. In a science the experimenter makes a prediction based on a hypothesis, which he/she has constructed as "new" knowledge in advance. However the process of discovering is of importance for learning. The student makes a prediction to which category an object belongs, what is the relationship between objects, how the object will change and what will happen after a certain time lapse. This process both develops knowledge consistent with reality and modifies wrong assumptions together with the training of the skills. Once the skill is proceduralized, it is possibly better remembered, because it is directly related to knowledge. The latter is meaningful because the student constructed it him/herself from reality, together with the development of a skill.

It now becomes clear the learning of knowledge and skills takes place jointly and that the find level (Merrill, 1983) is of importance in the acquisition of both. If the knowledge is constructed and the skill is proceduralized, then it can be used. This is Merrill's use level. The problems for finding a fact, categorizing an object, determining relationships or interpreting an event have their own typical procedure for solving it. A person can be skilled in the application of a certain procedure. The training of a skill without paying attention to the problem and the related knowledge means it is learned by rote. The problem no longer can be solved if it is redefined or changed somewhat.

The knowledge describes the regularities of the problem situation, or more general the regularities of reality. The label "rule" can be used to describe the regularities, e.g. a concept is a rule for classifying an object. Because the label can be applied to any regularity, both for the description of knowledge and procedures, it is not further defined and used here.

IMPLICATIONS FOR INSTRUCTION

The categorization and definition of knowledge and skills in the previous section has implications for designing instruction. The necessary steps for the design will be described, illustrated and discussed.

Define knowledge and skills, design problems

Before formulating the instructions for how to solve a category of problems, the teacher/instructor/designer who is the expert on the subject must define the category of problems and determine what the student should know and do. The teacher has to design problems which make it clear that the student has acquired the knowledge. Moreover he has to design problems, such that the student can demonstrate the skill.

Task analysis

The next task for the teacher is to solve a problem typical for the category and make a description of the sequence of operations, i.e. the problem solving procedure. This is the task analysis, which for every step in the analysis is accompanied by two questions for the designer to answer. First, on what knowledge is this operation based? Second, what is the prerequisite skill for carrying out this operation?

Presenting the knowledge and demonstrating the skill

After making the analysis the teacher prepares the instructional statements. Thus the teacher selects a best example of an object belonging to a certain category and specifies the procedure used to determine to which category an object belongs. Or the teacher selects two or more objects and specifies how to determine the relationship, or how, in case of change, to make a prediction.

Authentic activity

As soon as possible the students become active. The activity required should preferably be authentic. The teacher selects problems which preferably are real problems, solved by people who belong to a certain subculture.

Achievement test

The achievement test contains items for testing both the knowledge and the skills.

The main steps will be elaborated for the different kinds of knowledge and skills described in the previous section.

Class concepts

Suppose a biology teacher decides to design instruction on the concept "conifer". The teacher uses the following description: A conifer (1) is a tree (2) that has either needle leaves (3) or (4) scale leaves (3). This description of a class concept comprises the name of the object (1), the name of the universe (2), the relevant features (3) of the object and the sentential connective between the features (4). Because the concept is exclusive disjunctive, the two subsets, containing the elements, $(N \cap S')$ and $(N' \cap S)$ are taken for the selection of the best example. This is quite simple in this case and the teacher decides to give each student two branches of conifers, one with needle leaves and one with scale leaves. The instructor guides the inspection process and shows the relevant features, making use of a drawing. Moreover some irrelevant features get attention: evergreen, typical smell, rich in resin. The student's activity is authentic, like that of a botanist. To test whether the student is able to categorize based on the required knowledge, the student is asked to categorize a number of branches from both conifers and deciduous trees. Further categorization of conifers by family, genus and species requires a comparable identification procedure, but now more dimensions and values, e.g. form of leaf (needle, scale), form of fruit (cone, berry), color of fruit (red, blue), etc., are necessary. Learning to categorize depends on authentic activity. Correctly classifying means having acquired the knowledge. The non-botanist reader may realize that categorization of conifers is impossible without first having acquired the relevant knowledge. The conceptual or declarative knowledge is constructed based on the activity of categorization. The problem as such is simple to formulate: what is the name of this object or to which category does this object belong?

Sometimes discrimination of features is complicated. Take the following example of a class concept[1], taught in science. "An epithelial cell (1) is a cell (2) that lines the inside (3) or (4) the outside of an organ (3)". This concept again is a disjunctive concept. The teacher now has to decide how to isolate the relevant and irrelevant features and how to engage the student in authentic activity. First the teacher selects color transparencies, diagrams and prepared microscope slides to show the student a variety of types of cells: cuboidal, squamous (flat), columnar, stratified, etc., different in size and shape, but all having the feature of lining cells. Thus both relevant and irrelevant features are isolated. The student observes and inspects the slides. Then the teacher shows the students actual examples of epithelial cells in organs, e.g. from a fish and has the students prepare cross sectional slides. The teacher points out which ones are epithelial cells and which ones are not. Then the students make a skin scraping from the inside of his/her mouth to isolate an example of an epithelial cell. The latter activities are authentic.

To determine whether the use level is reached the teacher administers a test which contains items with various kinds of cells. The student has to determine which ones are epithelial cells. The use level is reached if the student correctly categorizes examples of epithelial cells from different organs.

The design of the necessary steps of the instruction for learning concepts is accompanied by secondary steps and features (Van Hout Wolters et al., this volume). Moreover, the designer will pay attention to the number of examples and the ratio of relevant and irrelevant features of examples (Leemkuil, this volume). The designer also will decide how to deliver the entire instruction: orally, written, computer assisted, using video, etc. Each medium has its own advantages and disadvantages in presenting the information, guiding the students' activity and supporting the learning process. The effect of video use is discussed by Ranzijn (this volume).

Relational concepts

The importance of the synchronization of the training of a skill and the construction of knowledge now is described for relational concepts. Suppose the task is to calculate a certain percentage of a given quantity. Carrying out the task is a skill. The task analysis (Gagné, Briggs & Wager, 1988) reveals the following subtasks: 1) To calculate a percentage of a given quantity divide that quantity by 100. (Or divide the percentage by 100). Write down the outcome. 2) Multiply the outcome of 1) by the percentage given. The outcome is the required result. The knowledge involved is a relational concept. It is described here as " a quantity, which is convenient to indicate a part-whole relationship ($A \subseteq B$)". One percent is 1/100 of a whole. For other subskills (addition, subtraction, multiplication and division) the knowledge of the set of real numbers is required. Of course, the teacher simply can state the relational concept for the students, but for real learning the student has to construct the knowledge in (authentic) activity. Thus different problems are presented in which the student has to construct a whole and a part. An example is shown in Figure 3.

The correct solution makes it clear that the student has acquired the knowledge. Another way to make clear that the student has acquired the knowledge is to ask for missing information. Take the following example.

"A hotel is cost effective if during each night 50% of the rooms are occupied. The Hengelo Crown Hotel had 7300 guests in 1988. Is the hotel cost effective?"

Mark 15 % of this area.
How many cm^2 is 15% of this area.

Figure 3. Example of a problem which has to be solved by constructing a relational concept.

Why can this problem not be solved? Because the numerical value of the "whole" is not known, further calculations are not possible.

A main rule for designing instruction for learning a problem solving procedure to find a relationship is to show a necessary step and to state why the step is and can be taken. By doing this the student's attention is focused to the knowledge part of the production system. Instructions in which a compiled procedure is shown will not be understood, which means that the student cannot acquire the knowledge. Take the following equation:

$$1 + x - 4 = 6 - 2x \tag{1}$$

The instruction to show the procedure for solving the problem: "Evaluate x", possibly will contain the following statements.

"An equation is a formula with two expressions connected by the equal sign. At least one of the two expressions has one or more free variables. In this case both expressions have the variable x. To find the value of the variable, first isolate that variable. This is usually done by isolating the variable on the left side of the equal sign and removing the variable on the right side. In (1) "-2x" has to be removed, which means change it to "0". This is done by adding "+2x". However, in doing this with one expression the two expressions no longer are equal and the same operation has to be done to the left side. Thus:

$$1 + x - 4 + 2x = 6 - 2x + 2x \tag{2}$$

Calculating the right expression yields

$$1 + x - 4 + 2x = 6. \tag{3}$$

An instruction like: "First bring the variable of the right expression to the left and change its sign" is instructing a compiled procedure, which is meaningless for a student and therefore an inappropriate instruction.

Class and relational concepts often become connected, based on the particular case which has to be described. In such cases the instruction contains statements, which clearly separate the concepts involved. The problems presented to the students for acquiring the knowledge and skills are formulated in such a way that the student either can construct the kn1jp173
owledge or retrieve it. The following example of a problem illustrates this.

"The University of Twente has a fund earmarked for visiting faculty, travel money for students and faculty, etc. Given that the annual spending amount (Dfl. 350 000) represents a 7% profit on capital, what is the capital administered by the board of the fund?"

Whether such a problem is used for acquiring the concept "percentage" or for learning to solve equations, it is difficult to solve for a beginning student. There are two relational concepts: "part-whole" and "equivalence". Percentage and equation are special cases of these concepts. Moreover the concepts are used to first specify an economic concept and further to set up an equation to solve the problem:

$.07x = 350\,000.$

The way in which a problem is formulated can help to promote the realization of the connection of the concepts. In the above-mentioned example the latter subordinate clause should be reformulated to "to which amount is the capital equal?" Hints can be given, like: "first try to find the unknown and assign the label of a variable, then set up a simple equation with one unknown quantity".

In designing problems for the purpose of knowledge acquisition and skill training the instructor first has to unravel which concepts the student has to connect. Then the problem can be written adequately.

Conditional concepts, scientific laws

In a scientific theory the change of "objects" is interpreted and future events are predicted. The description of the change and the interpretation of it comprise the knowledge. The analysis of the situation, the possible design of an instrumental procedure and the correct prediction of future events make up the skill. Take the following example of a well-known physical law.

"Most bodies expand if they rise in temperature." This phenomenon is interpreted by the molecular theory. If a body expands, the distance between the molecules increases. Molecules attract each other (potential energy). To realize a larger distance between molecules energy has to be transmitted to the body (increase of potential energy). To make this clear to the students the instructor will make a drawing of the assumed molecule structure and the internal forces to realize qualitative understanding and acquisition of knowledge.

A quantitative treatment of expansion often is done with solid bodies preponderantly expanding in one direction (pipes, railroad tracks, etc.). The expansion is called linear expansion. A student can make a calculation(prediction) of the expansion if the expansion coefficient, which is determined experimentally, is known. The prediction is made by applying the formula

$$\Delta l = \alpha * l_o * \Delta t$$

where
   Δl = change of length
   l_o = original length
   Δt = change in temperature (in ^{o}C)
   α = expansion coefficient

A more often used example is to calculate the necessary distance between railroad tracks to prevent warping in case of very warm weather. Example:
Given: $\alpha_{iron} = 11.7 * 10^{-6}/^oC$.
Suppose the railroad tracks are placed at a 20 ^{o}C temperature($t = 20$ ^{o}C). At this temperature the track has a length of 30 m. The tracks are anchored halfway. Now observe two pieces of 15 m belonging to one coupling. Further suppose the highest possible outside temperature is 40 ^{o}C.
The situation is shown in Figure 4.

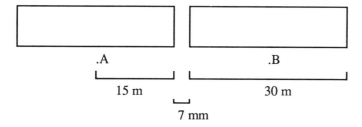

A,B = anchoring points

Figure 4. Illustration of distance between railroad tracks.

The solution of the problem:
   $\Delta l = 11.7 * 10^{-6} * 15 * (40 - 20)$
   $= 3.5 * 10^{-3}$ m
   $= 3.5$ mm.
Thus the opening between the tracks must be
   $2 * 3.5$ mm $= 7$ mm.

The general problem for the instructor in the case of teaching a lawful relationship, indicating a change and formulated as a conditional concept, is how to realize an instructive example or a problem in such a way to synchronize the knowledge construction and the learning and training of a skill. It is easily seen that the molecular theory is not directly connected to the quantitative treatment of the linear expansion of a solid body. Nor is the result of the calculation directly applied to a familiar physical situation and thus learning is not based on authentic activity. Nevertheless, because of its frequent use, students are able to imagine the example. Nearly all introductory physics textbooks use the example and show photographs of warped railroad tracks. A better example of authentic activity is achieved in physics education with simple direct current circuits being built by the student. In such an instructive environment the student can both construct the knowledge and make predictions about the current's behavior by making calculations. Predictions take on the form of calculations which in turn are based on quantitative relationships between physical concepts. A wrong prediction will cause "negative" feedback and possibly modification of existing knowledge. There are numerous situations in which for practical reasons learning through authentic activity becomes problematic, e.g. in case of demolishing equipment by making an error. In those situations, a demonstration is often given, a calculation is made, or the students practice with a *simulator* or a *simulation program*.

CONCLUSIONS FOR RESEARCH

The instructional design theory set up in the previous sections stresses the importance of knowledge acquisition through solving problems. The repeated solving of problems which may differ in context trains the skill and is necessary for its compilation and proceduralization.

The future research on instruction should study the effect of problem design on the construction of declarative and causal knowledge, the abstraction of knowledge to more general schemata, and the interaction between the construction of knowledge and the acquisition of the skill. Further questions should be addressed to the effect of (wrong) predictions on the modification of existing knowledge. Also attention should be paid to so-called qualitative conceptual knowledge, mental images of objects and their structure (prototypes). The problems should be constructed in such a way that authentic activity is possible and the synchronized development of knowledge and skills can be realized.

The study of these questions should be accompanied by research on presentation variables related to the subject matter and the task involved. Moreover, the potential of interactive media (in the form of simulations) to replace authentic activity will be the subject of research.

Note

1)   Example provided by G. Le Blanc, School of Education, Syracuse University.

REFERENCES

Anderson, J. (1982). Acquisition of cognitive skill. *Psychological Review*, *89*(4), 369-406.

Anderson, J. (1988). The expert module. In M.C. Polson & J.J. Richardson (Eds.), *Intelligent Tutoring Systems* (pp. 21-53). Hillsdale, NJ: Lawrence Erlbaum Associates.

Brown, J.S., Collins, A., & Duguid, P. (1989). Situated cognition and the culture of learning. *Educational Researcher, 18*(1), 32-42.

Collins, A., Warnock, E.H., Aiello, N., & Miller, M.L. (1973). Reasoning from incomplete knowledge. In D.G. Bobrow & A. Collins (Eds.), *Representation and understanding: Studies in cognitive science* (pp. 383-415). New York, NY: Academic Press.

Collins, A. (1977). Processes in acquiring knowledge. In R.C. Anderson, R.J. Spiro & W. Montague (Eds.), *Schooling and the acquisition of knowledge* (pp. 339-364). Hillsdale, NJ: Lawrence Erlbaum Associates.

Collins, A. (1988). Different goals of inquiry teaching. *Questioning Exchange: A Multidisciplinary Review, 2*(1), 39-46.

Gagné, R.M. (1965). *The conditions of learning.* New York: Holt, Rinehart and Winston, Inc.

Gagné, R.M., Briggs, L.J., & Wager, W.W. (1988). *Principles of instructional design.* New York: Holt, Rinehart and Winston, Inc.

Landa, L.N. (1983). The algo-heuristic theory of instruction. In C.M. Reigeluth (Ed.), *Instructional design theories and models* (pp. 163-211). Hillsdale, NJ: Lawrence Erlbaum Associates.

Merrill, M.D., & Boutwell R.C. (1973). Instructional Development: Methodology and Research. In F.N. Kerlinger (Ed.), *Review of research in education* (pp. 95-131). Itasca, IL: F.E. Peacock Publishers.

Merrill, M.D. (1983). Component display theory. In C.M. Reigeluth (Ed.), *Instructional-design theories and models* (pp. 279-333). Hillsdale, NJ: Lawrence Erlbaum Associates.

Merrill, M.D. (1987). The new component design theory: Instructional design for courseware authoring. *Instructional Science, 16,* 19-34.

Nicholls, J.G. (1984). Conceptions of ability and achievement motivation. In R. Ames and C. Ames (Eds.), *Research on motivation in education: Vol.1 Student motivation* (pp. 39-73). Orlando, FL: Academic Press, Inc.

Schank, R.C. & Abelson, R.P. (1977). *Scripts, plans, goals and understanding: An inquiry into human knowledge structures.* Hillsdale, NJ: Lawrence Erlbaum Associates.

Stillings, N.A., Feinstein, M.H., Garfield, J.L., Rissland, E.L., Rosenbaum, D.A., Weisler, S.E., & Baker-Ward, L. (1987). *Cognitive Science: An Introduction.* Cambridge, M.A.: The MIT Press.

AUTHOR INDEX

A

Abelson, R.P. 165
Adelson, B. 48, 93
Aiello, N. 173
Albert, J. 51
Algina, J. 143
Anderson, J. 48, 49, 63, 161, 163, 165
Arlin, M. 66
Atkinson, R.C. 142, 143
Atwood, M.E. 48
Austin G.A. 111

B

Baker-Ward, L. 163
Barfield, W. 48
Benjamin, Jr., L.T. 102
Berger, C.F. 46
Berliner, D.C. 63, 64
Biddle, B.J. 65
Bloom, B.S. 7, 8
Boutwell R.C. 159
Bovair, S. 94
Boyle, C.F. 49
Boyle, J.M. 96
Breen, T.J. 125
Breuer, K. 103, 108, 141
Briggs, L.J. 101, 157, 158, 170
Bromage, B. 48
Brooks, R. 49
Brophy, J.E. 65
Brown, J.S. 156
Bruner, J.S. 4, 14, 111

Bury, K.F. 96
Busemeyer, J.R. 125

C

Cahill, R.C. 80
Campbell, D.T. 69
Cantor, N. 113
Carroll, J.B. 7
Carter, K.J. 63
Carter, M.C. 80
Chao, J.N. 134
Christensen, B.R. 51
Christensen, D.L. 103, 106, 142, 145, 146
Clancey, M.J. 46
Clegg, C.W. 93
Clement, C. 46
Clements, D.H. 52
Cocchiarella, M. 112, 113, 124, 131, 135, 142
Cohen, J. 69
Coladarci, T. 76
Collins, A. 156, 165
Corbett, A. 49

D

Dalbey, J. 46, 97
Davis, C.E. 151
Day, D. 51
De Bruijn, I. 93
De Klerk, L.F.W. 124
De Weert, Ch.M.M. 80
Deck, J.G. 96

SUBJECT INDEX

ABOUT THE EDITORS

Sanne Dijkstra, University of Twente. Dr. Dijkstra is Professor of Education, University of Twente, working in the Division of Instructional Technology, Department of Education. Having received his Ph.D. in Psychology from Free University, Amsterdam, The Netherlands in 1974, his current research is centered in developing and testing instructional design rules for teaching problem solving and concept learning.

Bernadette van Hout Wolters, University of Twente. Dr. Van Hout Wolters is senior lecturer at the University of Twente, working in the Division of Instructional Technology, Department of Education. Having earned her Ph.D. in Psychology at Catholic University of Brabant, Tilburg, The Netherlands in 1986, her current work focuses on reading and learning strategies, self-instruction and designing instructional text.

Pieter C. van der Sijde, University of Twente. Dr. Van der Sijde is Program Co-ordinator for research on instruction at the Center for Applied Research in Education of the Department of Education, University of Twente. Since receiving his Ph.D. in Education from the University of Twente in 1987, his research interests have spanned the areas of teaching strategies, problem solving and instructional technology.

TEXAS A&M UNIVERSITY-TEXARKANA